P R E L I M I N A R Y

SUCCESS WITH **BEC**

HEINLE
CENGAGE Learning™

Success with BEC Preliminary Student's Book

Rolf Cook and Mara Pedretti with Helen Stephenson

Publisher: Jason Mann

Development Editor: Name Surname

Head of Media and Content Production: Alissa Chappell

Production Controller: Tom Relf

Compositor: Oxford Designers and Illustrators

Cover design: White Space

Illustrated by Gary Wing p19 and Phillip Burrows p52, p80 & p110.

ISBN: 978-1-902741-80-2

Heinle, Cengage Learning EMEA

Cheriton House, North Way, Andover, Hampshire, SP10 5BE
United Kingdom

Cengage Learning is a leading provider of customised learning solutions with office locations around the globe, including Singapore, the United Kingdom, Australia, Mexico, Brazil and Japan. Locate our local office at **international.cengage.com/region**

Cengage Learning products are represented in Canada by Nelson Education Ltd.

Visit Heinle at **http://elt.heinle.com**
Visit our corporate website at **www.cengage.com**

Acknowledgements

The authors would like to thank: Louis Garnade for his challenging invitation to write this book; David Riley for the long constructive talks; Karen Spiller for supervising the project and the editing; Liz Driscoll and Celia Bingham for their editorial work; and Stefania Bonuomo for reading and enjoying the original manuscript. We would also like to thank friends and students, who have been a great source of inspiration. Mara, in particular, would like to thank Davide for his valuable suggestions and constant support.

The publishers would like to thank Helen Stephenson for her valuable contribution to the project.

The publishers would like to dedicate the Success with BEC series to the memory of its inspirational editor, David Riley.

The publishers would like to thank and acknowledge the following sources for diagrams, copyright material and trademarks: Page 15 Reading test, Page 34 Listening test – Reproduced with the kind permission of Cambridge ESOL. Temping is learning – Reproduced with the permission of Quintessential Careers www.quintcareers.com. An agency built on proactive processes – Reproduced with the permission of www.redweb.co.uk. business2business: global communication – Reproduced with the permission of The Productivity Pro Inc. www.TheProductivityPro.com. No card, no ticket – Dear Editor – Based on article No Card, no ticket – Reproduced with the kind permission of Christopher Elliott. Creativity and Innovation – Based on article Simple ways to make yourself far cleverer by Denis Campbell. Copyright Guardian News & Media Ltd 2006. A business book review – Permission granted by Dupree Miller & Associates on behalf of Stedman Graham. Summertown Publishing would also like to acknowledge the Business English Certificates Handbook (published by University of Cambridge ESOL Examinations) as the source of exam formats and rubrics in the Exam Spotlight lessons and other exam-type activities throughout the book.

Every effort has been made to trace and contact copyright holders prior to publication; in some cases this has not been possible. We will be pleased to rectify any errors or omissions at the earliest opportunity.

Photography

Getty Images cover, pages 6, 7, 10, 11, 13, 16. McDonalds Media page 26. Easyjet page 28. Lastminute.com page 28. Bodyshop page 28. Getty Images pages 36, 39, 40, 46, 49, 53, 56, 62. Istockphoto.com page 66. Jumbo page 71. Hubdean page 76. Getty Images page 79. Smartlid Systems page 81. Honda page 86. Getty Images pages 90, 92, 93, 96, 101. CartoonStock page 107. Getty Images page 108. Google Logo (c) Google Inc. Reprinted with Permission page 109. Getty Images pages 112, 113. Photo Fusion page 116. Getty Images page 122. Commissioned photography Mark Mason pages 45, 84, 85, 114. Ian Lees page 80.

Summertown Publishing would like to thank the following for their contribution in reviewing Success with BEC in its early stage of production: Tessa Osborne, IFAGE Paroles, Switzerland Alwena Sullivan, The Canterbury School of English, IFAGE, Switzerland Amy Jost, International Companies, Switzerland Barbara Heck, Fachhochschule, Nordwestschweiz, Switzerland Caroline Häring, NSH Bildungszentrum, Switzerland Celeste Zappolo Berger, EB Zurich, Migros, SwitzerlandElizabeth Delbreil, International Companies, Switzerland Dr Holi Schauber, University of Fribourg, Switzerland James Stauffer, EasyEnglish, KPMG, PWC, MSJC, Switzerland Jayne Herzog, Klubschule, Migros, Switzerland Lilli-Marie Pavka, Zurich Business School (KV), Switzerland Norelee Wolf, Interlangues, Switzerland Reto Hähni, Flying Teachers, Switzerland Rosemarie Allemann, Univeristy of Applied Sciences, Switzerland Rudolf Weiler, KVZ Business School, Switzerland Sally Beale, IFAGE, The Canterbury School of English Sandy Egloff, PLSs, Switzerland Dave Davies, Asia Pacific Education, Cambridge ESOL Centre, Canada Louise Rankin, Communication Skills Consultancy, Norway Michael Williams, Fachhochschule Vorarlberg, Austria Otto Weihs, University of Applied Sciences, Austria James Schofield, Siemens, Germany

Printed by RR Donnelley, China
3 4 5 6 7 8 9 10 – 13 12 11

PRELIMINARY

SUCCESS WITH BEC

THE NEW BUSINESS ENGLISH CERTIFICATES COURSE

STUDENT'S BOOK

ROLF COOK AND MARA PEDRETTI

WITH HELEN STEPHENSON

Summertown Publishing

HEINLE
CENGAGE Learning

Australia • Brazil • Japan • Korea • Mexico • Singapore • Spain • United Kingdom • United States

CONTENTS

1.1 World of work

Training and workshops

1 J&C Training is a company providing training for other businesses. Look at the courses J&C Training offers and tick the ones that you find interesting. Compare with a partner and explain why the courses interest you.

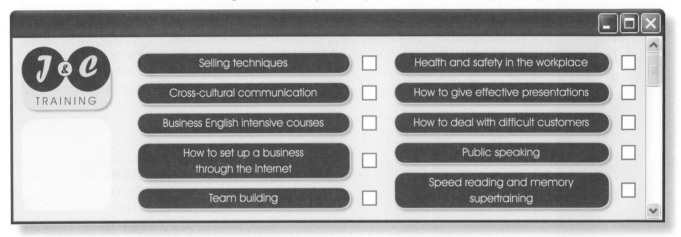

J&C TRAINING

- Selling techniques ☐
- Cross-cultural communication ☐
- Business English intensive courses ☐
- How to set up a business through the Internet ☐
- Team building ☐
- Health and safety in the workplace ☐
- How to give effective presentations ☐
- How to deal with difficult customers ☐
- Public speaking ☐
- Speed reading and memory supertraining ☐

2 Match the jobs (1–4) with their definitions (A–D).

1 an author
2 a speaker
3 a trainer
4 a consultant

A someone who talks at a public event
B someone who helps people to improve at a sport, skill or school subject
C someone who advises people on a particular subject
D someone who writes books or articles

3 Read this profile about the owner of J&C and fill the gaps with the jobs in exercise 2.

J&C TRAINING – about us

J&C is a training consultancy for personal and professional development in the workplace. It is based in Oxford and it is run by Janet Coyte.

Janet is an experienced teacher and **(1)** _____. She runs courses and workshops for companies and universities. As a **(2)** _____, she helps business people overcome difficulties. She sometimes gives one-to-one sessions on the phone or via email.

She is the **(3)** _____ of several books, and she writes articles on public speaking and presentation skills. Janet is also an internationally accredited public **(4)** _____, and she gives motivational talks around the world. Clients of J&C say that their courses are entertaining, professional and very practical.

4 Read the five sentences from emails sent to J&C Training. Which requests can J&C help with?

1 I want to study business English, but I can't travel to Oxford.
2 Our university department needs some IT training. Can you help?
3 I want to give a speech at my brother's wedding.
4 I'd like some help with writing a novel.
5 Our company would like some information on team-building weekends.

What does your job involve?

5 Five people from different companies are attending a J&C workshop on public speaking. Match their job titles (1–5) with their responsibilities (A–E). Write the correct letter A–E for each job.

Job titles

1 chief financial officer (CFO) _____

2 management consultant _____

3 personal assistant (PA) _____

4 quality manager _____

5 sales representative (rep) _____

Responsibilities

A visits customers, leaves samples and supports the customer service department.

B is responsible for testing new products and deals with customers' complaints.

C interviews clients and gives them advice.

D is responsible for the company's accounts, and controls money coming in and going out.

E organises meetings and deals with correspondence.

6 1.1 Listen to the five workshop participants introducing themselves. Complete the badges with the correct job title for each person.

7 Write two sentences which are true for you, using the expressions in exercise 5. Compare with your partner.

I deal with employees' problems.

The present simple

The present simple is used to talk about:

- permanent situations
  Q: *What **do** you **do**?*
  A: *I'm a sales rep. I **work for** a company that **supplies** computer software.*

- habits and frequency of activities
  Q: ***Do** you often **travel** abroad?*
  A: *Yes, I **go** to Italy two or three times a month.*

- timetables (with a time expression)
  Q: *When **does** your train **leave**?*
  A: *It **leaves** at 14:45.*

I **Complete the sentences with the present simple form of the verbs in brackets.**

1 'What _____ your company _____?' (produce)
   'It _____ electrical appliances.' (make)

2 'How many people _____ you _____?' (employ)
   'We _____ 1,200 employees.' (have)

3 '_____ you _____ your goods abroad?' (export)
   'Yes, we do. We _____ all over Europe.' (ship)

4 'How often _____ you _____ staff meetings?' (have)
   'Once or twice a month. We _____ them every week.' (not hold)

5 'What time _____ the meetings _____?' (start)
   'They usually _____ at 11 o'clock.' (begin)

6 '_____ Peta _____ you with your work?' (help)
   'Yes, she does, but she _____ a lot of time.' (not have)

Adverbs and expressions of frequency

We often use these adverbs of frequency with the present simple:

always   usually   often   sometimes   rarely   never

Adverbs of frequency usually go:
- before most verbs *She **often** prepares Power Point presentations.*
- after the verb *be* *He is **never** late.*

We also use expressions such as *once a week, twice a month, every Monday, on Thursdays*. These usually go at the end of the sentence.
*We have a staff meeting **every Monday** / **on Mondays** / **once a week**.*

2 **Put the words in the correct order to make sentences.**

1 meetings / month / we / every / have / two

   _____

2 December / bonus / always / in / gets / a / he

   _____

3 rarely / complaints / we / receive / any

   _____

4 produce / catalogue / year / every / new / we / a

   _____

5 she / schedule / behind / is / never

   _____

Work–life balance

3 Do you work or study too much? Or do you know how to balance your work with your life? Take this test to find out. Answer the questions by writing a number (0–5).

PERSONALITY QUIZ

HOW OFTEN ...

0 = never
1 = seldom / rarely
2 = occasionally
3 = frequently / often
4 = usually / normally
5 = always

1 do you plan your day's activities? ☐

2 do you sleep eight hours a night? ☐

3 do you find time to relax during the day? ☐

4 are you on time for appointments? ☐

5 do you spend more than an hour on lunch? ☐

6 do you see your friends at weekends? ☐

7 do you do exercise or sports during the week? ☐

8 do you read a magazine in the evening? ☐

9 do you wake up full of energy in the morning? ☐

10 do you laugh in a normal work day? ☐

TOTAL SCORE ☐

HOW TO INTERPRET THE SCORE:

41–50: Well done! You find it very easy to relax. But be careful – you are so relaxed that you are in danger of disappearing! Maybe you need to wake up and make sure people still know that you are there.

31–40: You find it quite easy to relax. People like being with you, because you are a positive presence.

21–30: You don't find relaxing very easy and life is a bit difficult for you.

11–20: You don't find relaxing easy at all – that's why you struggle so much at home and at work.

10 or below: You're making life hard for yourself – and maybe for the people around you too. Your health may even be suffering. Relax!

Exam Success

In Part Two of the Speaking Test, you will give a short presentation. There are two topics and you have to choose one of them. The heading on the topic sheet is *What is important when ...?*

4 Work in pairs.

Student A: Interview your partner using the questionnaire above.
Student B: Give as much information as you can.

A: Do you plan your day's activities?
B: Yes, I usually plan my day's activities the night before. I write appointments in my diary.
A: How often do you see your friends?
B: I see them once a week. We have supper together every Friday night.

5 Work in pairs. What things are important in maintaining a work–life balance?

1.2 Personal and professional details

Meeting people

1 Here are some phrases you can use when you greet somebody. Choose the best response (A–G) for each phrase (1–6).

0 Good morning. My name's Ros Cox.
1 Hello. I'm Lothar Muller.
2 Excuse me. Are you Linda Gordon?
3 Hello, Ms Leonardi. How are you?
4 Excuse me. Is your name Brown?
5 Hi, George. Nice to see you again.
6 Pleased to meet you, Mr Lehman.

A Not too bad, thanks. And you?
B No, I'm not.
C Pleased to meet you, Ms Cox.
D How do you do, Mr Muller?
E Please, call me Peter.
F Yes, it is.
G Nice to see you too.

2 Work in pairs to check your answers. Then practise saying the greetings and responses.

3 In which of the situations in exercise 1 are the people meeting for the first time?

4 Complete the conversation with the sentences in the box.

It's a real pleasure to work with her.	Nice to meet you, Ian.
Do you know her?	May I introduce myself?
My boss is in Sydney.	She's in Singapore, too.

Ian   Hello. (**1**) _____ My name's Ian and I work in the Asia–Pacific division.

Henry   (**2**) _____ My name's Henry and this is my colleague, Sarah.

Sarah   Hello, Ian. Do you work in the Sydney office?

Ian   No, not at the moment. (**3**) _____ But I'm based in Singapore.

Henry   Look! There's Michelle over there. She's based somewhere in Asia. I can't remember where exactly. (**4**) _____

Ian   Yes, we're on the same project this year. (**5**) _____

Henry   Ah, lucky you. She's really beautiful – and clever too.

Ian   Yes, I know. (**6**) _____

Sarah   Well, I think I'll leave you boys to discuss ... work.

Henry   Oh, Sarah, you're not jealous, are you?

Sarah   No, I'm not ... Michelle, how lovely it is to see you again.

5 🔊 1.2 Listen to the conversation and check your answers.

Personal and professional profiles

6 Find out about your classmates, using the questionnaire. First, work in pairs and prepare questions. Then interview your classmates and record the numbers.

0   Do you have a hobby?

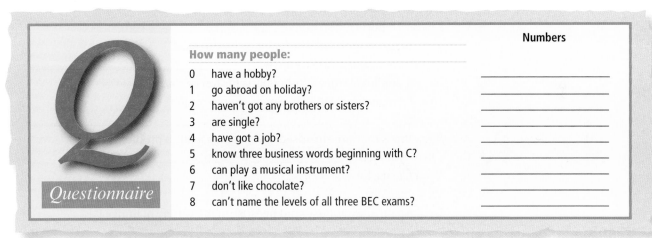

Q

Questionnaire

How many people:	Numbers
0 have a hobby?	_____
1 go abroad on holiday?	_____
2 haven't got any brothers or sisters?	_____
3 are single?	_____
4 have got a job?	_____
5 know three business words beginning with C?	_____
6 can play a musical instrument?	_____
7 don't like chocolate?	_____
8 can't name the levels of all three BEC exams?	_____

7 Work with a new partner. Interview each other. Fill in the fact file with information about your partner.

Fact file

Name _____   Hobbies _____

Surname _____   Family _____

Town _____   Job title _____

Favourite destination for holidays _____

Reasons for learning English _____

8 With your partner, work with another pair of students. Introduce your partner to the other people in the group, using the information in exercise 7. Listen to the other presentations. Ask a follow-up question to each person.

Do you like living in ...?

9 Write a personal profile of your partner. Use the information from the fact file in exercise 7, but include one false sentence. Write 30–40 words.

10 Swap profiles with your partner. Read the profile about you and find the false sentence.

job and *work*

1 Kostas Hadavas is a PA in a company that provides catering services. It's an unusual job for a man, so the in-company magazine interviews him. Write the correct form of the questions.

SPOTLIGHT ON STAFF

0 Q: What / name? What's your name?
  A: Kostas Hadavas.

1 Q: How / spell / surname? _____
  A: H-A-D-A-V-A-S.

2 Q: What / do? _____
  A: I'm the personal assistant to the managing director of Athens Daily Menu.

3 Q: Who / managing director? _____
  A: His name's Georgos Solomos.

4 Q: What / your job / involve? _____
  A: I deal with clients, and I organise meetings and events.

5 Q: / write / reports too? _____
  A: Yes, I often write reports and memos for our staff.

6 Q: / work / only in the Athens area? _____
  A: No, we don't. We work in other parts of Greece too.

7 Q: How / people / react to you, a man, doing this job?
  _____
  A: Sometimes they are surprised, but it isn't usually a problem at all.

8 Q: / like / your job? _____
  A: Yes, I like it a lot.

9 Q: Why / like / it? _____
  A: Because I'm always busy, and because of the variety of things I do.

Learning Tip

Make a note of the questions you got wrong. Try to analyse why you made the mistakes. Repeat the exercise next week and see if you improve.

2 🔘 1.3 Listen to the conversation and check your answers.

3 Use some of the information from the interview to write a profile of Kostas Hadavas for the magazine. Write 30–40 words.

4 Work in pairs to fill the gaps with *job* or *work*. Which word is both a verb and a noun? Which word is only a noun?

1 It's an unusual _____ for a man.
2 'What's your _____?' 'I'm an electronics engineer.'
3 We _____ with several Asian companies.
4 Many students have a part-time _____ to earn extra money.
5 My brother starts his first _____ on Monday. He's very nervous about it.
6 Where do you _____ these days?
7 She always does a great _____ when she organises events.
8 It's my _____ to welcome visitors and show them around.
9 I like my new _____. The _____ is varied and interesting.
10 'Hi, Steve. Are you still at _____?' 'Yes, I'm still in the office.'

5 Work in pairs.

Student A: Write a list of jobs usually done by women.
Student B: Write a list of jobs usually done by men.

Compare your lists and think of three areas where traditions are changing.

6 Rowan Barker Tate Inc. is a multinational confectionary company. Every year, at the annual meeting, the company awards a prize to its 'Employee of the Year'. Work in groups of four. Allocate one candidate (A–D) to each student in the group. Then read the criteria and the information about your candidate and decide why he/she should win.

ROWAN BARKER TATE INC.

Employee of the Year Award

Employee
of the Year

The employee should:
- make a significant contribution to company efficiency, profit, product development or staff development.
- deal with professional or personal problems successfully.
- be a mentor or set a positive example to others.
- represent the company values of healthy living.

This year's candidates are:

A

B

C

D

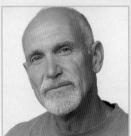

Ian Rogers is 40 years old. He's a production manager and he's based in Singapore. His responsibilities are to supervise projects and to coordinate resources. His professional background is in engineering.
Ian usually goes scuba diving at weekends and he also enjoys marathon running and cooking. He runs a sports club for local children and he raises money for their training.

Michelle Yong is 36. She's a finance assistant and she's based in Singapore. Michelle usually deals with Asia division accounts and sometimes does auditing for other divisions. She has a master's degree in business administration.
In her free time Michelle likes painting, and she also does judo. Michelle suffers from Chronic Fatigue Syndrome and often works from home, but this does not stop her ambitious career plans.

Sarah Mullen is 31 years old and based in the head office in Dallas. As the company's communications director, she deals with the company's internal and external communications. Sarah is also in charge of the company's successful new email system. She regularly works late to help colleagues or to attend external events. Sarah has a degree in journalism.
Sarah's personal interests are writing detective stories, breeding Yorkshire terriers and showing her dogs in exhibitions.

Henry King is 57 and is the research and development manager. Henry is based in Dallas. He manages R&D of new product ideas, including the best-selling new chocolate chewing gum range. Henry is famous for always thinking of new ideas and projects.
Henry's professional background is in food technology, and in his free time he enjoys visits to museums, art galleries and the theatre.

7 Discuss the four candidates in your groups and choose a winner.

Useful language

I like Ian best. He …
Michelle should win because she …
I think Sarah is the best candidate. She …
I think Henry should win because …

1.3

BEC Preliminary Exam

Exam Success

What are your strong and weak areas in English? Concentrate on the areas you have most difficulty with at first.

The BEC Preliminary Exam has three papers and tests your reading, writing, listening and speaking skills.

Each skill is worth 30 marks (total = 120). The pass grade is around 65% (or around 80 marks). You pass or fail on your total marks. For example, if you fail one skill but your total is 90, you pass the exam.

The table below shows the length of each test and its structure. You will learn more about the structure of each test in this book.

Paper	Skill(s)	Marks	Length (minutes)	Structure
1	Reading & Writing	30 + 30	90 minutes (Reading: 60 minutes Writing: 30 minutes)	Reading: 7 parts Writing: 2 parts
2	Listening	30	40 minutes	4 parts
3	Speaking	30	12 minutes	3 parts

You will get your results approximately seven weeks after the exam. Your results show your overall grade (*Pass with Merit, Pass, Narrow Fail* or *Fail*) and your performance in each paper. If you pass, you will get your certificate about four weeks after your results.

❙ **Read about the format of the BEC Preliminary Exam above. Find the answers to these questions.**

1 How many papers are there in the BEC Preliminary Exam? _____

2 What skills are tested? _____

3 What's the maximum number of marks you can get? _____

4 How many marks do you need to pass? _____

5 Do you have to pass all four skills to pass the exam? _____

6 Which is the longest paper: Reading & Writing, Listening or Speaking? _____

7 How many parts are there in the Reading Test? _____

8 How many parts are there in the Speaking Test? _____

9 When do you get your results? _____

10 What do the results tell you? _____

11 When do you get your certificate? _____

12 Does everyone get a certificate? _____

Reading Test

The Reading Test has seven parts, which are always in the same order:

- Parts One to Five test your general reading comprehension.
- Part Six tests your grammar.
- Part Seven tests your ability to complete a form with relevant information.
- Each part contains a reading text and a comprehension task.
- Many different types of text are used, such as notices, messages, adverts, timetables, leaflets, graphs, charts, business letters, product descriptions, reports, minutes, newspaper and magazine articles, memos. Column 4 in the table below shows which text types are used in each part of the exam.
- You have 60 minutes to answer 45 questions and to transfer your answers to the Answer Sheet in pencil. If you need to change an answer, use an eraser.
- You can make notes on the text but not on the Answer Sheet.
- The table below summarises all the features of the Reading Test.

Part	Questions	Task type	Text type	Example
1	5	Multiple choice	Notices, messages, timetables, adverts, leaflets, etc.	Unit 5, page 54
2	5	Matching	Notice, list, plan, contents page, etc.	Unit 5, page 54
3	5	Matching	Graphs, charts, tables, etc.	Unit 5, page 55
4	7	Right / Wrong / Doesn't say	Advert, business letter, product description, report, minutes, etc. (150–200 words)	Unit 9, page 94
5	6	Multiple choice	Newspaper or magazine article, advert, report, leaflet, etc. (300–400 words)	Unit 9, page 95
6	12	Multiple choice cloze	Newspaper or magazine article, advert, leaflet, etc. (125–150 words)	Unit 12, page 124
7	5	Form-filling, note completion	Short memos, letters, notices, adverts, etc.	Unit 12, page 125

2 **Read about the format of the Reading Test above and decide whether the following statements are true or false. Tick ✓ as appropriate.**   **True**   **False**

1 There are five parts in the Reading Test. ☐ ☐
2 Grammar is not tested in the Reading Test. ☐ ☐
3 A wide variety of text types are used. ☐ ☐
4 Graphs and charts containing figures are used as texts. ☐ ☐
5 There are 45 questions in each part of the test. ☐ ☐
6 You have 60 minutes to do the Reading Test. ☐ ☐
7 You must write your answers in pencil. ☐ ☐
8 You can't make notes on the Reading text. ☐ ☐
9 The longest text has 300–400 words. ☐ ☐
10 All the tasks are multiple choice. ☐ ☐

Work in progress

New projects

1 2.1 **Listen to the telephone conversation between Vicky and Steve. Steve is calling from Brazil. What is their relationship?**

2 2.1 **Listen to the conversation again and choose the best ending (A, B or C) for each sentence (1–4).**

1 Steve is calling from
   A his office.   B the shops.   C a hotel.
2 Steve is in Fortaleza because he's
   A got friends there.   B working there.   C travelling around Brazil.
3 Vicky is
   A having lunch.   B watching TV.   C gardening.
4 The children are
   A fighting.   B at school.   C playing.

3 Can you remember what Steve is doing in Brazil? Read this email to his business partner and check your answer.

From: Steve Lenzer
To: Louise Bernard
Subject: Update from Brazil
Date: 22 May

Hi Louise,

We're very lucky to have this construction contract in Brazil. It's a pity that I'm only here for a week, but that's business. Anyway, let me update you on my visit here.

The construction of the Belém Panorama is going well and guests will love it! Apart from some minor problems, everything is proceeding according to plan. They're now building the swimming pool on the 12th floor. The local staff are working very well with our management team.

I'm working in Fortaleza today and tomorrow. The new shopping centre is quickly taking shape: there are no problems and I think we're ahead of schedule. They're doing a great job here too.

I'm flying back to Britain at the weekend, so I'll see you in the office on Monday.

Best wishes,

Steve

Exam Success

This exercise is similar to Part Four of the Reading Test. Choose 'Wrong' when the sentence contradicts information in the text. Choose 'Doesn't say' when the information is not mentioned.

4 Read the email again. Decide whether these sentences are 'Right' or 'Wrong'. If there is not enough information to choose 'Right' or 'Wrong', choose 'Doesn't say'.

1 Steve is in Brazil for work.
   A Right   B Wrong   C Doesn't say
2 The Belém Panorama is a hotel.
   A Right   B Wrong   C Doesn't say
3 There was a problem with the floors of the Belém Panorama.
   A Right   B Wrong   C Doesn't say
4 The construction of the shopping centre is behind schedule.
   A Right   B Wrong   C Doesn't say
5 Steve is staying in Brazil until Monday.
   A Right   B Wrong   C Doesn't say

The present continuous

The present continuous is used to talk about:

- an action that is happening now, at the moment of speaking
  Q: *What **are** you **doing**?*
  A: *I'm **checking** the financial report.*

- an ongoing action which is happening around this time
  *The local staff **are working** very well with our management team.*

- a temporary activity
  *A temp **is helping** out this month.*

- a fixed arrangement in the future
  Q: *Are you **coming** to tomorrow's meeting?*
  A: *No, I'm sorry. I'm **leaving** for Lisbon tomorrow morning.*

5 Read Steve Lenzer's email again. Underline all the verbs in the present continuous. Which verbs are examples of a fixed arrangement in the future?

6 Complete the sentences with the present continuous form of the verbs in brackets.

1 The CEO and the CFO _____ (discuss) the company's current projects.

2 Jane _____ (give) a presentation of the new line we _____ (launch) next month.

3 Mark _____ (make) some photocopies in the shop across the road.

4 Lisa _____ (talk) about the opening of the new branch in Japan.

5 We _____ (have) a small party today at 4pm to say goodbye to our marketing manager, Rob, who _____ (leave) at the end of the month.

7 Louise Bernard gets an email from project manager, Carlos Gutierrez. Complete the email with the correct form of the verbs in the box. What are the differences between this project and the Brazil project?

| fly have meet not follow take |

From: Carlos Gutierrez
To: Louise Bernard
Subject: Update from Spain
Date: 23rd May

Hi Louise,

Just to update you on the project here in Valencia. We (**1**) _____ some problems, I'm afraid.

The local manager (**2**) _____ the building plans and everything is behind schedule.

I (**3**) _____ the subcontractors this afternoon – I need to know why everything

(**4**) _____ so long. I hope to get some answers!

I (**5**) _____ to London on Tuesday evening. See you on Wednesday.

Best regards

Carlos

1 Read the text about temping below. Choose the best answer (A, B or C) for each question (1–4).

IF YOU ARE EVER in a period of transition, when you are not working in your usual career field – or if you don't have enough experience to get a permanent job in the area you are interested in – working for a temporary employment agency can be a great way to earn money, get more experience, and try out different kinds of work.

When you temp, the agency sends you to work at client companies for anything from a few hours to a few months, sometimes even longer. The reasons why companies need temps vary. When small companies are growing quickly, for example, or are developing short-term projects, they don't want to contract permanent staff. And when a staff member is taking maternity leave, employing a temp is also a good option for the company.

The people who temp, on the other hand, often enjoy it because the routine changes from day to day. There are other advantages. 'If you don't know what career field you want to work in, temping can help you find some answers,' says Eliane Facet, who runs a temp agency in Montpellier, France. 'As a temp, you might discover some fields you definitely don't want to work in. Not all of our temps have lots of experience. Right now, ten business students from our agency are working in different companies. They are experiencing the things they are learning about at college. They are improving existing skills, and also learning numerous others.'

From her own experience of temping, Eliane says, 'After long jobs, I used to send thank-you notes to the supervisors, telling them what I liked about working with them. Whenever I did this, the agency told me how happy the company was with my work, and then gave me better jobs.'

1 Which of the following statements is true?
   A Temp agencies always send temps to the same company.
   B Temps always do the same kind of work.
   C Temping jobs do not always last the same length of time.

2 According to the text,
   A there are different reasons why businesses need temps.
   B permanent staff are a good option for small companies.
   C temporary staff usually do routine jobs.

3 According to the text, temping gives you the opportunity
   A to take long holidays.
   B to get work experience.
   C to meet a lot of people.

4 When you finish a temporary job, it is a good idea
   A to tell your supervisor what you think of him/her.
   B to let the company know what was good about the experience.
   C not to say anything – you don't want to hurt anyone's feelings.

2 Find words or phrases that mean:

1 time of change (after the end of one job and before the beginning of the next (paragraph 1) _____ _____ _____

2 area of work (paragraphs 1 and 3) _____ _____

3 time off to look after your baby (paragraph 2) _____ _____

4 people who check that you are working correctly (paragraph 4) _____

Temporary jobs

3 Work in pairs. Read these comments about temping. Are they positive or negative comments? Tick ✔ as appropriate. Then add your own comments.

		Positive	Negative
A	It's very uncertain. You never know when you will be working and when you won't.	☐	☐
B	I really love the variety of going to different companies.	☐	☐
C	You work with different levels of management.	☐	☐
D	It's difficult when you don't get clear guidance from the client company.	☐	☐
E	I enjoy meeting different people all of the time.	☐	☐
F	The first day in a new job is always quite frightening.	☐	☐
G	_____	☐	☐
H	_____	☐	☐
I	_____	☐	☐

VOCABULARY

Hiring and firing

4 Work in pairs. Look at the pictures and write the correct verb form in each gap.

5 Choose the appropriate words to complete the sentences.

1 The company is giving *a pay rise / a pay cut* to employees who meet their targets.

2 There's a lot more administration work with this project; we need to *employ / dismiss* more office staff.

3 Their sales are dropping, so they are *taking on / sacking* about 10 per cent of the workforce.

4 The department is *hiring / firing* employees who are performing badly.

2.2 Making arrangements

Arranging a meeting

1 🔘 2.2 It's Friday morning. Martina Möller is calling Dave Prakash to arrange a meeting. Listen to their conversation. When do they agree to meet?

Day _____ Time _____

2 🔘 2.2 Work in pairs. Listen to the conversation again.

Student A: Write in Martina's diary what she is doing next week.
Student B: Write in Dave's diary what he is doing next week.

Martina

Monday, 18
am   visit new plant
pm _____
Tuesday, 19
am _____
pm _____
Wednesday, 20
am _____
pm _____
Thursday, 21
am _____
pm _____
Friday, 22
am _____
pm _____

Dave

Monday, 18
am _____
pm   take time off
Tuesday, 19
am _____
pm _____
Wednesday, 20
am _____
pm _____
Thursday, 21
am _____
pm _____
Friday, 22
am _____
pm _____

3 Now tell your partner the information you have written in your diary.

Student A: Tell Student B what Martina is doing next week.
Martina's visiting the new plant on Monday morning.
Student B: Fill in Martina's diary.

Student B: Tell Student A what Dave is doing next week.
Dave's taking time off on Monday afternoon.
Student A: Fill in Dave's diary.

4 Read Martina's email to Dave Prakash. Choose the best 'Subject' line (A, B or C).

A Plans for the weekend
B Meeting next week
C Visit to the new plant

To: Dave Prakash
Subject: _____
Hi Dave,
I'm just writing to confirm our meeting next Wednesday. I've booked a table at the Italian restaurant in Grey Street. It's quite quiet, so we can talk.
I'll see you in Reception at 12.30.
Have a good weekend!
Martina

5 Look at these questions from the conversation between Dave and Martina. Tick the suggestions.

When can we meet? ☐
How about Monday morning? ☐
Are you free on Thursday? ☐
Are you going to the trade fair? ☐
What about Tuesday, for lunch? ☐
How does 12.30 sound? ☐

Confirming a meeting

6 Look at the list of activities below and choose three to do on Monday. Write them on the diary page and add another two activities of your own.

Memo
- present company to potential client
- meet sales team
- have lunch with Mark
- show quality inspectors around
- meet marketing manager
- visit production plant
- interview job applicant
- collect kids from school

MONDAY, 18

8AM _____ 1PM _____

9AM _____ 2PM _____

10AM _____ 3PM _____

11AM _____ 4PM _____

12AM _____ 5PM _____

7 Work with a partner. Using your diary page in exercise 6, arrange to meet on Monday.

8 Write an email to your partner to confirm your meeting. Use the email in exercise 4 to help you.

To:
Subject:

Prepositions of time: *at, in, on*

We use *at, in* and *on* with the following time expressions:

- *at* + specific times, festivals in general; also *at lunchtime, at night, at the weekend*
- *in* + parts of the day, months, seasons, years, centuries
- *on* + days of the week and parts of named days, named festival days, dates

Note: *at the weekend* (UK English) and *on the weekend* (US English).

1 Fill the gaps with *at, in* or *on*.

0 in 2009
1 _____ Christmas
2 _____ winter
3 _____ seven o'clock
4 _____ June
5 _____ the afternoon

6 _____ the evening
7 _____ New Year's Day
8 _____ 20 July
9 _____ the 21st century
10 _____ Friday morning
11 _____ half past six

2 Fill the gaps with the correct prepositions.

1 The design meeting is _____ Friday _____ 4.30.
2 We opened our Buenos Aires office _____ 2003. We're opening a second office _____ September.
3 I'm flying to Washington _____ Wednesday next week. My return flight is _____ 16 May.
4 I'm going to lunch now. Can I speak to you _____ the afternoon?
5 I don't have time to write the report today. I'll do it _____ Monday morning.
6 I'm self-employed. I find I often work best _____ night.

Accepting an invitation

3 Look at the letter. Who is it to? Who is it from?

New Directions
Osborne Park
Morpeth

May 2nd 20___

Dear Mr Olaya

4 The sentences in the letter below are in the wrong order. Put them into the correct order (1–6).

_____ I look forward to seeing you again this year.

_____ Please confirm your attendance at both the fair and the reception.

_____ This year, the fair is taking place at the new convention centre in Morpeth, on 21st and 22nd June.

_____ You are also invited to a special reception at 8pm on 21st June, to celebrate the tenth anniversary of New Directions and our new venue.

_____ Best regards, Andrea Greer

_____ I am writing to invite you to the New Directions Book Fair in June.

5 Bob Olaya and Felix Lund of Menta Books are talking about the Book Fair. Complete the conversation with prepositions of time.

Bob   Felix, are we planning to go to the New Directions Book Fair this year?

Felix   Yes, I think so. It's always a good event. We usually make lots of new contacts. When is it?

Bob   It's (**1**) _____ June this year. It's (**2**) _____ Thursday and Friday the 21st and 22nd.

Felix   Oh, just a second. Aren't we going to Helsinki that week?

Bob   No, the Helsinki conference is (**3**) _____ July.

Felix   Oh yes, that's right. Fine, let's go to the Book Fair.

Bob   There's a special reception (**4**) _____ the 21st.

Felix   Is it (**5**) _____ lunchtime?

Bob   No, it's (**6**) _____ the evening (**7**) _____ 8 o'clock.

Felix   Sounds great! Can you get everything organised?

Bob   No problem. I'll confirm our attendance.

6 🔘 2.3 Listen to the conversation and check your answers.

7 Write a reply to Andrea Greer to confirm your attendance at the fair and either accept or decline the invitation to the reception. Use some of the expressions from the Useful language box below in your letter. Write 60–80 words.

Andrea Greer
New Directions
Osborne Park
Morpeth

May 7th 20___

Dear Ms Greer

Useful language	
Thank you for …	We will be delighted to …
Many thanks for …	It will be a pleasure to …
We can confirm …	I'm very sorry, but …
I confirm our …	I regret that …

2.3

Writing Test

The Writing Test comes immediately after the Reading Test. You have 1 hour and 30 minutes to do the Reading and Writing Tests.

The Writing Test has two parts:

In Part One, you have to write a piece of internal communication, ie to someone in the company. You have to write 30–40 words.

In Part Two, you have to write a piece of business correspondence, ie to someone outside the company. You have to write 60–80 words.

You write both answers on the Answer Sheet.

There is a total of 30 marks for the Writing Test.

EXAM PRACTICE

Exam Success

During the exam, you must write your email on the Answer Sheet provided. The information for **To**, **Date** and **Subject** is given. You don't need to copy this onto the Answer Sheet.

1 **Answer the exam question below.**

- You are going to take your BEC Preliminary Exam.
- Write an **email** to your teacher:
  - telling her that you are preparing for the exam
  - asking her for more information about the Writing Test
  - asking her for any suggestions on how to avoid mistakes.
- **Write 30–40 words.**

To:	Ms Dilts
From:	
Date:	6 February
Subject:	Information on BEC Preliminary Exam

---

2 **Read your teacher's reply. Which paragraph (1–5) is about the following?**

A Part One of the Writing Test _____

B Part Two of the Writing Test _____

C avoiding mistakes _____

From:	Jane Dilts
To:	
Date:	7 February
Subject:	RE: Information on BEC Preliminary Exam

(1) I'm glad to hear that you're going to take the BEC Preliminary Exam.

(2) In the exam, you must produce two pieces of writing: the first is an internal company communication and the second is a piece of business correspondence.

(3) The first might be a note, a message, a memo or an email of 30–40 words. The register (the language style) can be neutral or informal. There are written prompts (instructions) for this part of the Writing Test.

(4) The second piece of writing might be an email, a letter or a fax of 60–80 words. In this task, you will have to give information about a product, deal with requests, make or change reservations, apologise, complain, etc. This kind of communication is always with somebody outside the company and is written in reply to an email, letter or fax from this person. The register is either neutral or formal.

(5) Remember to read your writing several times to check structure, content, grammar, vocabulary and spelling.
Good luck in the exam.
Best regards,
Jane Dilts

---

3 Read the teacher's reply again and decide if the following features are connected with Part One or Part Two of the Writing Test. Tick ✔ as appropriate.

	Part One	Part Two
1 internal communication	☐	☐
2 business correspondence	☐	☐
3 30–40 words	☐	☐
4 60–80 words	☐	☐
5 note	☐	☐
6 letter	☐	☐
7 informal	☐	☐
8 formal	☐	☐
9 written prompts	☐	☐
10 reply	☐	☐

4 Correcting mistakes is an essential skill for writing. Read the memo below, which a student has written in the exam. Circle any mistakes and write the appropriate correction symbol above them.

Correction symbols:

Grammar	G	Spelling	Sp
Wrong Word	WW	Punctuation	P
Word Order	WO	This meaning is not clear	?

- You are going to attend a three-day training course.
- Write a **memo** to your boss:
  - saying that you will be out of the office
  - telling him when you are coming back
  - reminding him that one of your colleagues will deal with the new temp.
- **Write 30–40 words.**

M E M O

To: Jeff Hutchinson

From:

Date: 21 May

Subject: Training Course

Hi Jeff,

I'm going to a(ttend) [Sp] a training course on selling techniques for tree

day, so I'm not going to be in office.

I'll be back on Mondays, 27th May.

Remind that tomorrow a temp is start Deborah will show her what

to do.

3.1 Company biography

1 Work in pairs. Do you like fast food? When was the last time you went to a fast food restaurant? What do you like about fast food restaurants? What do you dislike?

2 Read the text about how one man transformed a small restaurant into a global business. Find the following information.

1 the place of the original McDonald's restaurant
2 what was on the original McDonald's menu
3 the names of the owners of the original McDonald's
4 who developed the McDonald's franchise
5 how many McDonald's restaurants there are today

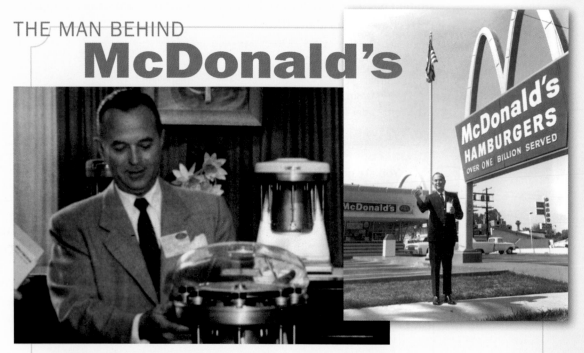

THE MAN BEHIND McDonald's

IN 1954, TWO BROTHERS ran a small, but busy, restaurant in San Bernardino, California.

The restaurant featured a limited menu that included: hamburgers, french fries, soft drinks and milkshakes. The milkshakes were very popular and the restaurant had purchased ten special "Multimixer" milkshake makers. Each one could mix five milkshakes at a time.

A salesman named Ray Kroc was the exclusive distributor of the "Multimixer" milkshake machines at that time. Ray decided to visit the restaurant; he wanted to find out why they had so many machines.

Ray talked to Richard and Maurice (Mac) McDonald, the owners of the restaurant. He saw how they prepared the food using equipment that they had invented. The service in the restaurant was fast and the prices were inexpensive.

Ray realised that this was a fantastic opportunity. He wanted to open more restaurants and so sell more multimixers.

In April 1955, Ray opened his first franchised McDonald's restaurant in Des Plaines, Illinois. First day sales were $366.12.

Ray continued to franchise new restaurants and to expand. In 1961, he bought the business from the MacDonald brothers for $2.7 million.

Today, McDonald's Corporation has over 31,000 restaurants in over 100 countries. There is even one in Kuwait City, which opened in 1994. On its first day, there were 15,000 people lining up to eat at the restaurant.

3 Read the text carefully. Choose the best ending (A, B or C) for each sentence

1 In 1954, Richard and Maurice
  A ran a hamburger restaurant.
  B didn't like milkshakes.
  C prepared the food by hand.

2 Ray Kroc
  A owned a restaurant in California.
  B invented a milkshake maker.
  C sold machines for making milkshakes.

3 Ray opened
  A his first restaurant in California.
  B his first restaurant in Illinois.
  C his first restaurant in 1961.

4 When a restaurant opened in Kuwait City, it was
  A not very busy on the first day.
  B quite busy on the first day.
  C extremely busy on the first day.

GRAMMAR

The past simple

> In the affirmative form, regular verbs end with -ed: *talk – talked, play – played, stop – stopped, study – studied, travel – travelled, prefer – preferred.*
>
> For irregular verbs, such as *speak – spoke, tell – told,* you have to learn the forms.

4 Look at the reading text. Underline all the verbs in the past simple. Decide which are regular and which are irregular. Write the infinitive and the past simple forms in a table in your notebook. Compare with your partner.

Regular verbs		Irregular verbs	
infinitive	past simple	infinitive	past simple
feature	featured	run	ran

> The past simple is used:
> - to talk about actions that happened in the past. The time is specified, or understood from the context.
>   *Ray **talked** to the owners.*
> - to talk about past states.
>   *In 1954, two brothers **ran** a small restaurant.*

5 Work in pairs. How much do you remember about McDonald's? Ask each other these questions. Then look at the text again to check your answers.

1 Where was the original restaurant owned by the McDonald brothers?
2 What did it sell?
3 Was it expensive?
4 When did Ray Kroc open the first McDonald franchise?
5 How much money did they take on the first day?
6 How much did Ray Kroc pay the brothers for the business?
7 When did the Kuwait City restaurant open?
8 Was the Kuwait City restaurant a success?

Company profiles

1 Work in pairs. Write three things you know about each of these companies.

2 Complete the text with the correct form of the verbs. Which company in exercise 1 does this text describe?

Anita Roddick and her husband Gordon got the idea for their business in 1970, when they
(**1**) _____ (visit) a natural cosmetics store in San Francisco. Back in England, they (**2**) _____ (begin) producing their own naturally-inspired cosmetics and they (**3**) _____ (open) their first shop in 1976. The products and the shop's philosophy (**4**) _____ (be) revolutionary for the time. The Roddicks (**5**) _____ (buy) the raw materials direct from the producers, and they (**6**) _____ (pay) their Community Trade suppliers a fair wage. Today, The Body Shop continues to bring ethical trade to the high street in more than 55 countries.

3 Complete the text with the correct form of the verbs in the box. Which company in exercise 1 does this text describe?

> be become begin not / have not / own sell not / sell take

Stelios (**1**) _____ the first two aircraft he operated. He (**2**) _____ tickets through Travel Agencies and he (**3**) _____ any company employees. Everything was contracted from other companies. It was 1995, and it (**4**) _____ the beginning of a revolution in air travel. Just three years later, the company (**5**) _____ the first online air ticket, it (**6**) _____ services outside the UK and it (**7**) _____ delivery of its own fleet of planes. When it merged with another low-cost airline, Go, in 2002, it (**8**) _____ Europe's biggest budget airline.

4 Work in pairs. Use the prompts to write questions about lastminute.com. Do you know the answers to any of these questions?

1　Brent Hoberman and Martha Lane Fox / the company (start)
　Where _____?
2　the website (sell)
　What _____?
3　the company (expand into)
　Which countries _____?
4　they / after six years (have)
　How many employees _____?
5　the company (go public)
　When _____?
6　Martha / the company (leave)
　When _____?

5 🔊 3.1 Listen and write the answers to the questions in exercise 4.

1 _____　　3 _____　　5 _____

2 _____　　4 _____　　6 _____

Presenting your company

6 Decide whether these types of business organisations usually have one owner (O) or more than one owner (M).

1 a freelancer _____

2 a non-profit organisation _____

3 a public limited company (plc) _____

4 a sole trader _____

5 a limited company (Ltd) _____

6 a partnership _____

7 self-employed _____

7 Do you see yourself as a 'dot.com millionaire' or a celebrity entrepreneur? Work in pairs to design your own company, choosing one of the types of business organisation in exercise 6. Complete the first column of the table with your company biography.

	Your company biography	Your partner's company biography
Company name		
Type of company		
Product / Service offered		
Got idea for business in … (when)		
First business activity (when / where)		
Expanded (where to / when)		
Notable successes		
Key dates / achievements		
Current operations		
Number of employees		
Current value of company		
Current personal worth		

8 Practise giving a spoken presentation about your company, using the notes you made in exercise 7.

9 Now present your company to a new partner. While you listen to the presentation, complete the second column of the table above with as much information as you can about this company. Ask follow-up or clarification questions as necessary.

10 Use your notes to write a short paragraph (60–80 words) about your company. You will not need to use all of the information. Choose the most relevant, interesting or unusual facts. Before you start, read the paragraphs about The Body Shop and easyJet again. Follow a similar organisation in your paragraph.

11 Work with your partner from exercise 7 again. Exchange your paragraphs and compare them. Did you choose the same information to write about?

3.2

Company performance

What companies do

1 Write the names of as many companies you can think of in one minute. Compare with your partner.

2 Which of these verbs can you use to describe the activities of your companies in exercise 1?

design   sell   distribute   provide   manage   publish   market
export   import   produce   supply   organise   manufacture

Armani designs and sells fashionable clothes.

3 Look at the press releases. What event is each company announcing? Choose from the following?

A a new CEO   B record profits   C a new product
D a new contract   E new shops

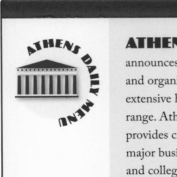

ATHENS DAILY MENU
announces a new line in vegetarian and organic menus, to add to its extensive high-quality product range. Athens Daily Menu provides catering services for major businesses, hospitals, schools and colleges, using only quality ingredients to prepare tasty and nutritious menus. The company supplies meals for over 15,000 people every lunchtime! With an efficient, high-quality catering service Athens Daily Menu can help any organisation to improve its image, and make financial savings. They also provide catering for special occasions, from banquets for up to 1,000 people to romantic dinners for two.

SISSO is pleased to announce the signing of a major new deal with a Japanese car manufacturer. The deal guarantees the future of both SISSO plants and is a symbol of SISSO's growth philosophy. SISSO manufactures innovative, high-quality seats and interiors for cars, sport utility vehicles and vans. SISSO designs its components in close conjunction with the client, guaranteeing satisfaction. With clients in both Europe and the USA, SISSO exports up to half of its production.

4 Fill in the fact file using information from the texts.

	Athens Daily Menu	SISSO
Products / Services		
Customers		
Other information		

Press release

5 Use the information below to write a similar press release for another company. Write 60–80 words. Read your partner's text and make one suggestion for improvement.

Company name – Soap Heaven
Products / Services – soaps, shampoos and skin-care goods
Customers – teenagers – male & female, Western Europe
Other information – a new CEO is joining the company; ambitious expansion plans into new EU markets

Company structure

6 3.2 Nigel Parker is presenting his company to a new potential business partner. Listen to his presentation. What is the company's core business?

7 3.2 Listen to the presentation again and complete the organisational chart.

Learning Tip

When you study on your own, always listen to the recording at least twice.

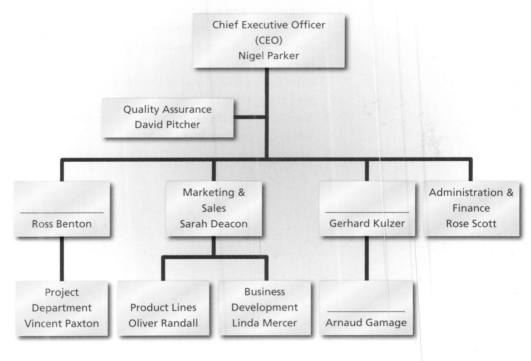

PARKER ELECTRONIX

Exam Success

In Part Three of the Listening Test, you listen to a monologue and complete gaps with one or two words. Practise listening and making notes to help you with this.

8 Decide whether the following statements are true (T) or false (F).

1 The company is based in the north of England.
2 The founder of the company was Nigel's uncle.
3 It was founded in 1960.
4 Its latest product is a new optical instrument.
5 It has 70 employees.
6 Parker Electronix has a turnover of $7.5 million.

9 3.2 Listen to the presentation again and check your answers.

Production, sales and share prices

1 Work in pairs. Match the words in the box with the arrows.

decrease   drop   fall   go up   increase   level off   rise   remain steady

A

_____
_____
_____

B

_____
_____
_____

C

_____

D

_____

2 Look at graphs A–F below. Choose the appropriate words to complete the sentences.

A Production *dropped / rose* steadily in the second half of the year.

B When I was away, production *fell / increased* dramatically.

C Sales *dropped / went up* sharply after the product was advertised on TV. Everybody wanted it!

D Sales *decreased / rose* after Christmas, but fortunately they went up steadily in the following months.

E The share price *decreased / increased* steadily, but then it *levelled off / remained steady* during the summer.

F Our share price *levelled off / remained steady* for the whole of last year.

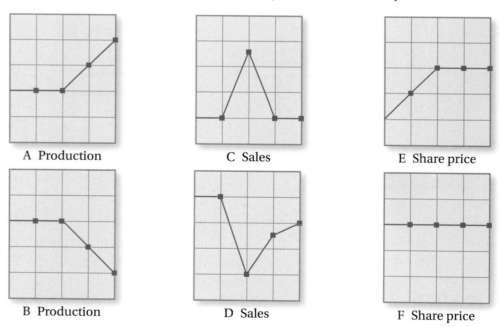

A Production   C Sales   E Share price

B Production   D Sales   F Share price

3 3.3 Listen to the CEO of Plaksa Plastics giving a summary of the annual report. Choose the correct graph for production, sales and share price.

4 Draw similar graphs for the company you invented on page 29. Prepare a spoken presentation to explain the graphs. Work in groups of three. Present your company results. Try to speak for one minute.

5 Read the extract from a company brochure. Who is it written for?

A potential investors
B potential staff
C a new CEO

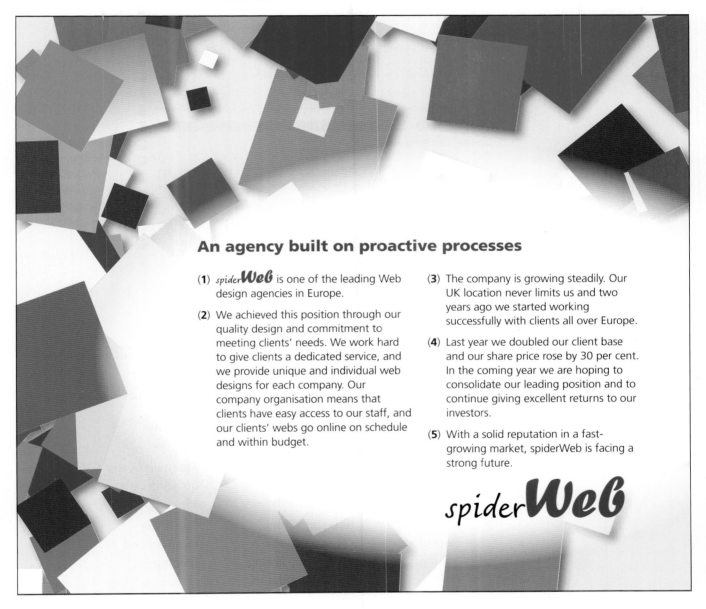

An agency built on proactive processes

(**1**) *spider***Web** is one of the leading Web design agencies in Europe.

(**2**) We achieved this position through our quality design and commitment to meeting clients' needs. We work hard to give clients a dedicated service, and we provide unique and individual web designs for each company. Our company organisation means that clients have easy access to our staff, and our clients' webs go online on schedule and within budget.

(**3**) The company is growing steadily. Our UK location never limits us and two years ago we started working successfully with clients all over Europe.

(**4**) Last year we doubled our client base and our share price rose by 30 per cent. In the coming year we are hoping to consolidate our leading position and to continue giving excellent returns to our investors.

(**5**) With a solid reputation in a fast-growing market, spiderWeb is facing a strong future.

*spider***Web**

6 Read the extract again and answer these questions

1 Where is the company based?
2 Where do its clients come from?

7 Use the information about the company you invented on page 29 to write the first section of your company brochure. Follow the format of the spiderWeb brochure. Write about 80 words.

3.3 Listening Test

The Listening Test lasts 30 minutes. You then have 10 minutes to transfer your answers to the Answer Sheet.

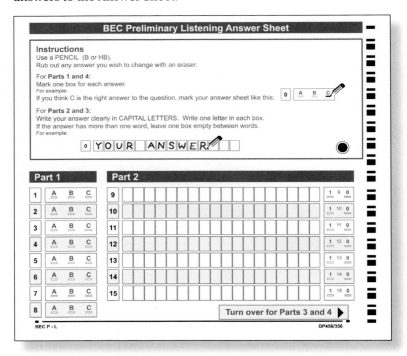

There are two types of listening:

- **listening for gist** – the general meaning of a text
- **listening for specific information** – usually numbers (dates, times, percentages, prices, etc) or spellings

You will hear each monologue or conversation twice. The total mark you can get is 30.

Part	Main skill focus	Input	Response	Number of questions
1	Listening for specific information	8 short conversations or monologues lasting 15–30 seconds	Multiple choice questions, with 3 options	8
2	Listening for specific information	Short telephone conversation or monologue lasting about 1½ minutes	Gap filling – numbers and spellings	7
3	Listening for specific information	Monologue, lasting about 2 minutes	Note-taking	7
4	Listening for gist / specific information	Conversation, interview or discussion between 2 or more people, lasting about 3 minutes	Multiple choice questions, with 3 options	8

Read about the format of the Listening Test above, including the Answer Sheet. Will the Answer Sheet for Parts Three and Four be the same as for Part One or Part Two?

Listening Test: Part One

2 🔘 3.4 **Answer the exam questions from Listening Part One below. Read the instructions and Exam Success before you listen to the recording. Follow the instructions and write your answers on the Answer Sheet on the opposite page.**

• For questions **1–8** you will hear eight short recordings.
• For each question, mark one letter (**A**, **B** or **C**) for the correct answer.
• You will hear the eight recordings twice.

1 When did Janet send the letters?
  A 13 June
  B 30 July
  C 14 June

2 Which training course do they choose?
  A Negotiation Skills
  B Presentation Skills
  C Computer Skills

3 What are the opening times of the factory outlet on Thursday?
  A 9.00am – 6.15pm
  B 9.00am – 7.50pm
  C 9.00am– 7.15pm

4 Which logo does Janet prefer?

  A   **B**   **C**

5 Where is the stand located at the exhibition?
  A Hall J, stand No. 18
  B Hall A, stand No. 80
  C Hall H, stand No.18

6 How many visitors were there at this year's exhibition?
  A 50,312
  B 15,312
  C 15,311

7 Which slide is correct?

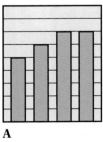 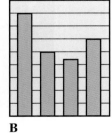 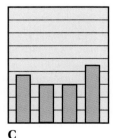

  A   **B**   **C**

8 How many more bottles do they need?
  A 20
  B 100
  C 120

4.1 International business

READING

1 Work in pairs. Write down ten classroom objects or things you have with you. Where was each thing made? How many were imported?

2 Write three things your country imports and three things it exports. Compare with another pair. Where do the imports come from?

3 Tick the words you know. Check the others in a dictionary.

> producer   wholesaler   customer   retailer   warehouse
> consumer   competitor   customs   port   clothing

4 Fill each gap in these sentences with a word from the box above. Then compare your sentences with a partner.

1 Rotterdam is the biggest _____ in Europe.
2 A _____ sells products direct to the public.
3 Your business rival is your _____.
4 A _____ is the 'end user' of goods.
5 Japan is a major _____ of electrical goods such as audio products.
6 A _____ is a place where things are kept before they are sold.
7 There is no _____ control between EU countries.
8 A _____ buys from manufacturers and supplies retailers.

5 Read the newspaper article about imported clothes and find six of the words from the box in exercise 3. (Some of the words are in the plural.)

Fashion industry crisis after EU import ban

THE FASHION INDUSTRY in Europe is facing its biggest crisis in recent history. Clothing retailers such as H&M, Zara and C&A could have empty shops at Christmas because Chinese imports are stuck in European ports. At the moment, millions of Chinese bras, sweaters and T-shirts are sitting in customs warehouses around Europe, following the introduction of import controls in June by the European Trade Commissioner, Peter Mandelson.

A spokeswoman for the retailers said that many small companies are suffering because they cannot sell these Chinese imports. 'People could lose their jobs and small retailers are facing huge losses,' said Anna Price. 'The EU should release these goods as soon as possible, in time for the Christmas season.'

On the other hand, countries such as Italy, Spain and Portugal are in favour of the import restrictions. These countries employ many people in the textile industry. They don't want Chinese clothing to flood the market because they can't compete with Chinese prices.

Mr Mandelson is in a difficult position; maintaining the controls could be a disaster for the retailers. But allowing the imports could be equally disastrous for the southern European producers. Meanwhile, the warehouses are filling up with winter season fashions which nobody will want next winter.

6 Decide whether these sentences are 'Right' or 'Wrong'. If there is not enough information to choose 'Right' or 'Wrong', choose 'Doesn't say'.

1 The European fashion industry is the biggest in the world.
   A Right   B Wrong   C Doesn't say

2 Some European clothing companies sell clothes to China.
   A Right   B Wrong   C Doesn't say

3 Retailers can't buy Chinese imports at the moment.
   A Right   B Wrong   C Doesn't say

4 Some EU countries agree with the import controls.
   A Right   B Wrong   C Doesn't say

5 Chinese clothes are cheaper than clothes produced in Europe.
   A Right   B Wrong   C Doesn't say

6 Mr Mandelson is taking a decision on the crisis this week.
   A Right   B Wrong   C Doesn't say

7 Compare your answers with a partner. For the questions that you have answered 'Right' or 'Wrong', which words helped you to decide the answer? For the questions you answered 'Doesn't say', why did you give this answer?

LISTENING

Views on import controls

8 4.1 Listen to the radio news item and decide whether each of the two speakers is for or against the import controls.

9 4.1 Listen to the news item again and correct the mistakes in these sentences. Compare with a partner. Which speaker do you agree with?

1 Joao da Silva owns a clothing shop in Aveiro.
2 He supplies a small number of people.
3 His message is 'support European exports'.
4 Dagmar Rasmussen is happy with the situation.
5 Tulip's shops are already empty.
6 Dagmar says that the Trade Commissioner should resign.

10 Do you know what happened next? Think of two possible endings.

11 4.2 Listen to the rest of the news item to find out if you are right.

SPEAKING

Imported goods

12 H&M buy 30 per cent of their clothing from China, and 70 per cent of shoes sold in the UK are imported. In pairs, discuss why a European company decides to import goods. Use these ideas. Can you add any of your own?

The quality of the goods is better.
It's difficult to find European manufacturers.
The price is lower.
Foreign designs appeal to Europeans.
The goods are made very quickly.
Other countries can supply in large quantities.

Modal verbs: *can/could* and *should*

Modal verbs have the same form for all subjects. The negative form ends with *n't* and the modal verb goes before the subject (*I*, *he*, etc) in questions.

- We use *can* to talk about present ability and possibility.
  *I **can** speak English and Spanish.* (ability)
  *He **can't** finish the work before he goes home.* (possibility)
- We use *could* to talk about future possibility and past ability.
  *Our shops **could** be empty next week.* (future)
  *I **couldn't** speak to him yesterday.* (past)
- We also use *Can/Could I/we* when asking for permission and making offers. We use *Can/Could you* in requests.
  ***Can I** leave early this evening?* (permission)
  *How **can I** help you?* (offer)
  ***Could you** sign this form for me?* (request)
- We use *should* to make recommendations, and to ask for and give advice.
  *The European Union **should** protect European industry.* (recommendation)
  *You **shouldn't** be rude to customers.* (advice)

1 **Look at the words in brackets in the table above. Write the correct word next to each sentence below.**

0 Can we use our dictionaries during the exam?   *permission*
1 Could you spell your surname, please?   _____
2 Students should attend all their classes.   _____
3 I can't do any of these questions. They're too hard.   _____
4 You shouldn't stay up late the night before the exam.   _____
5 She could be the best candidate for the job.   _____
6 I couldn't speak to Mr Jones because he was in a meeting.   _____
7 Can I show you what to do?   _____
8 How fast can you type?   _____

2 **Complete the sentences with *can*, *can't*, *could* and *couldn't*.**

1 You _____ smoke here. If you smoke, the alarm goes off.
2 I'm afraid Mrs Doriguez isn't available at the moment. _____ you come back later, please?
3 '_____ you read this dossier for tomorrow?' 'No, I'm sorry, I _____.'
4 Good morning, Johnson & Johnson. _____ I help you?
5 Mr Jensen is not in at the moment. _____ I take a message?
6 I _____ call you because the battery of my mobile was flat.

3 **Work in pairs. Take turns as Student A and Student B in each of these situations.**

Student A: Choose one of the problems below. Tell your partner about it.
Student B: Listen to your partner's problem and give him/her some advice.

- You have just sent an email full of spelling mistakes to an important client.
- Your colleague is often late for meetings with suppliers and it reflects badly on the company.
- Your boss can't keep his records organised and it gives you lots of extra work.
- You can't speak any other languages, but you want to be promoted.
- Your colleague is often away from his desk for long periods and you have to make excuses for him.
- You never remember clients' names and it is embarrassing.

4 What advice would you give someone who was arranging a teleconference?

5 Read the article from an in-house magazine and check your ideas.

business2business: global communication

Teleconferencing is a great way to connect people who work in different parts of the world. It's cheaper and quicker than face-to-face meetings, and people can communicate more informally, sitting in their offices or even working from home.

If you want your teleconference to be effective, you should plan it like a face-to-face meeting. First of all, find a date that's convenient for everyone. Remember time differences, and be careful to specify the local time of the virtual meeting: New York is five hours behind London, so if you want a teleconference with someone in New York, the best time is probably after 2pm in London. Limit the number of participants – managing a teleconference with more than five people can be stressful. Before the meeting, send out the agenda so that everybody knows the topics for discussion. Send all participants the documents for the meeting.

The person who calls the meeting is usually also the 'moderator'. Before you speak, always say your name – 'This is Stephanie' – so that everybody knows who is saying what. Silence on the phone doesn't mean absence. Maybe someone is preparing a question or thinking of an answer. And here is another tip. When you're not speaking, press the 'mute' button so that you can listen to who's talking, but the others won't hear your background noises.

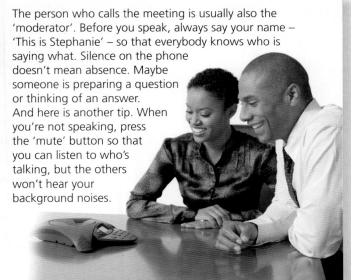

6 Read the text again and choose the correct ending (A, B or C) for each sentence (1–4).

1 Teleconferencing is ideal if

  A you want to work with people from different parts of the world.

  B you want to be effective in meetings.

  C you don't have time for face-to-face meetings.

2 When it's 2pm in London, the time in New York is

  A 7am.   B 9am.   C 9pm.

3 Before anyone speaks, they should

  A say 'This is Stephanie'.

  B say the name of the person they want to talk to.

  C identify who they are.

4 Press the 'mute' button when

  A you are talking to the other people.

  B you want to listen to what people are saying.

  C you are not participating in the teleconference.

7 Match words from A and B to make collocations from the article.

A	B
1 connect	the agenda
2 face-to-face	differences
3 work	a teleconference
4 time	people
5 manage	meetings
6 send out	a question
7 prepare	from home
8 press	the 'mute' button

8 Write questions with collocations. Then ask your partner the questions.

How often do you have face-to-face meetings at work?

4.2 Business communications

On the phone

1 Work in pairs. Read each phrase and decide who could say it – the person who makes the call (C) or the person who receives the call (R)?

1 Can I help you?
2 Can I leave him a message?
3 Can I say that back to you?
4 Does she have your number?
5 I'd like to speak to ... , please.
6 I'll call back later.
7 I'll ask ... to call you when she gets back.

8 I'll give it to you.
9 I'll pass your message on to ... .
10 I'm sorry, the line is busy.
11 This is ... , of ... .
12 Who's calling, please?
13 Would you like to leave a message?
14 I'm afraid ... is not in her office at the moment.

2 Match what the receptionist says (1–6) with the caller's responses (A–F). Then practise saying the short exchanges with your partner.

Receptionist	Caller
1 Smith & Sons. Can I help you?	A No thanks. I'll call back later.
2 Who's calling, please?	B Thank you very much. Goodbye.
3 Can I take a message?	C Hello. I'd like to speak to Albie Smith, please.
4 Does he have your number?	D Can I leave him a message?
5 I'm sorry. The line is busy.	E It's Jane Bowman of Bowman's Builders.
6 I'll ask him to call you when he gets back.	F I'll give it to you now.

3 4.3 Listen to the telephone conversation between Jane Barrett of Bryant & Sons and the receptionist at Wates' Office Supplies. Underline the objects that Jane mentions.

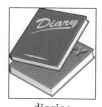

printer cartridges   pencils   pens   envelopes   paper   diaries

4 4.3 Listen to the conversation again. Complete the order form with the correct letters and numbers.

Office Supplies

Order Form		
Quantity	*Description*	*Model*
3	**(a)** boxes of _____ paper	
(b) _____	printer cartridges	**(e)** _____
(c) _____	boxes of pencils	
(d) _____	boxes of pens	

Tel: 0573 – **(f)** _____

5 Work in pairs. Practise the telephone conversation, following the pro...

Receptionist	Caller
You work for Thorpe Office Supplies Ltd. Answer the call.	
	Ask to speak to Raj Kahn.
Say that Mr Kahn is in a meeting. Offer to take a message.	
	Explain that your order has arrived and it is wrong. You ordered: four diaries, three packets of envelopes, and two printer cartridges. You received: one diary, six packets of envelopes, and one printer cartridge. The printer cartridge was the wrong one.
Ask which printer cartridge the customer ordered.	
	Code: HL630
Ask which printer cartridge the customer received.	
	Code: HPC 3903 A
Say that you will ask Mr Kahn to call when his meeting finishes. Ask if he has the customer's telephone number.	
	Give your number.
Say the number again to check it.	
	If the number is correct, say so.
Say that you will pass the message on.	
	Thank the receptionist. Say goodbye.

WRITING

Exam Success

This is similar to the task in Part Two of the Writing Test. You have to write a response to a short communication. Don't copy from this text: practise ways of writing the information in your own words.

Dealing with complaints

6 Read this section of a letter from a customer to Mr Raj Kahn. What is the main purpose of the letter? Choose from the following.

A to return an order
B to complain about the non-arrival of an order
C to cancel an order

Dear Mr Kahn,

I am writing to complain about our stationery order of 12th March. Following my telephone conversation to your office on 21st March, I expected to receive the correct goods. However, that was a week ago and we are still waiting for delivery.

Could you please assure me that the order will be sent correctly and as soon as possible? If not, we will be forced to look for another supplier in the future.

Yours sincerely,

Peter Paxman

7 Reply to the customer, apologising for the problems and giving an explanation. Offer the customer a discount of 5 per cent on the order. Write 60–80 words.

Useful language	
I apologise for ...	We had a problem with ...
Please accept my apologies for ...	I would like to offer ...
I would like to apologise for ...	I can offer ...
Unfortunately ...	Please accept ...
The problem was due to ...	

will for offers and promises

> We often use *will* when we decide to do something – for example, in offers and promises.
>
> *I'll ask him to call you.* (offer)
> *I'll do it later.* (promise)

1 Complete the sentences with *I'll* and a suitable verb.

1 Mr Grey isn't in his office. _____ him you rang.

2 I know Carrie's extension number. _____ her for you.

3 _____ at these accounts today, I promise.

4 Those files look heavy. _____ them for you.

5 I pass the post office on my way home. _____ those letters for you.

6 I'm not usually late. _____ at work on time tomorrow!

2 Complete the conversation below with the sentences in the box.

I'll write the report tomorrow morning.	I'd like to check them again.
I'd like to speak to Natalia Marin, please.	I'll see you tomorrow.
I'll send them to you this afternoon.	Would you like to come?

Natalia Westlaine Pharmaceuticals.

Sven Hello. (**1**) _____

Natalia Speaking.

Sven Hi, Natalia. It's Sven. I need your budget figures for the report. Can you email them to me?

Natalia They're not ready yet, I'm afraid. (**2**) _____
Some of the figures aren't quite right.

Sven When do you think they'll be ready?

Natalia I'm working on them now. (**3**) _____
Is four o'clock alright?

Sven Yes, that's fine. (**4**) _____

Natalia Oh, by the way, Margareta is leaving next week. We're having a little party tomorrow afternoon. (**5**) _____

Sven Yes, I'd love to. What time?

Natalia Half past three.

Sven Great. (**6**) _____ Bye.

3 🔘 4.4 Listen to the conversation and check your answers.

4 Practise the conversation with a partner.

5 Work in pairs. Use the prompts below to practise conversations with your partner. Each exchange will involve making an offer, a promise or a request.

1 **Retailer:** The delivery of new plasma screen TVs is late. Your special promotion starts tomorrow.
Wholesaler: Promise to find out why there is a problem.

2 **Exporter:** You need prices and schedules for a shipment of electrical equipment to Mexico.
Freight forwarder: Ask if the exporter wants the information by fax or email.

3 **Distributor:** You want to know when the merchandising products will be available.
Manufacturer: Offer to find out and return the call.

4 **Wholesaler:** You want to know if your containers have arrived.
Importer: Ask if the wholesaler wants to speak to the warehouse.

Telephone messages

6 4.5 **Listen to extracts from four telephone conversations and tick the expressions you hear.**

How do you spell that? ☐
Could you spell your name, please? ☐
M for Madrid. ☐
Did you say the 21st? ☐
Let me just check that. ☐
Could you repeat that, please? ☐

7 4.6 **Listen to four telephone calls and correct two mistakes in each message.**

1

Reid, Whelan & Blake

Telephone Message

Message for: _Ms Chandra_
From : _Joe Panetta_
Caller's company: _AC Associates_
Tel./Email: _0632 157431_
Message: _Would you like to_
wait for the new brochure which is
coming out in two weeks' time?

2

Reid, Whelan & Blake

Telephone Message

Message for: _Mrs Horbaczewski_
From : _Bob Davis_
Caller's company: _____
Tel./Email: _bd.davis@hotmail.com_
Message: _Could you post_
Mr Davis a copy of his tax form for
last year?

3

Reid, Whelan & Blake

Telephone Message

Message for: _Mrs Peters_
From: _Sigrid Junge_
Caller's company: _Hoffmann gmbh_
Tel./Email: _____
Message: _Can you see Ms Junge_
on the 16th? She can't fly to London
on the 17th.

4

Reid, Whelan & Blake

Telephone Message

Message for: _Mr Dando_
From: _Martin Kramer_
Caller's company: _____
Tel./Email: _____
Message: _He hasn't accepted_
the first offer.

8 4.7 **Listen to three short recordings. Choose the best answer (A, B or C) for each question.**

1 When will the goods arrive?
 A on 3 February   B on 16 February   C on 19 February

2 Who does the caller want to speak to?
 A the personnel manager   B the production manager   C the managing director

3 What new time does the caller suggest for the meeting?
 A 1.00pm   B 2.30pm   C 4.30pm

4.3

Speaking Test

The Speaking Test lasts 12 minutes in total. It has three parts and you can get 30 marks. You do the Speaking Test with a partner.

Part One is an interview. This is a conversation between an examiner and each candidate. It lasts about two minutes in total. The topics for conversation could be: giving personal details, talking about your work or studies, describing your home, speaking about your hobbies, etc. You also have to give your personal opinions.

Part Two is a mini-presentation. Each candidate chooses one topic. You have one minute to organise your thoughts and one minute to present your ideas. At the end, the other candidate has to express his/her opinion of your ideas and you have to do the same. The topics for your presentation could be: choosing a course, booking a flight, selling a new product, etc. In total, this part lasts five minutes.

Part Three is a discussion. In this part of the test, the examiner presents a situation using pictures or a text. You then have a conversation with the other candidate, discussing ideas and making choices. The examiner asks you to explain your choices. The topics for discussion here could be: training, health and safety, business services, management skills, etc. The third part lasts five minutes in total.

1 **Read about the Speaking Test above and decide if candidates do the following in Part One, Part Two or Part Three. Tick ✔ as appropriate. Some of the features are connected with more than one part of the test.**

	One	Two	Three
1 You might look at pictures.	☐	☐	☐
2 You have time to prepare what to say.	☐	☐	☐
3 You talk about yourself.	☐	☐	☐
4 You choose what to talk about.	☐	☐	☐
5 You answer the examiner's questions.	☐	☐	☐
6 You discuss a situation with your partner.	☐	☐	☐
7 You talk for a minute about a subject.	☐	☐	☐
8 You comment on what your partner has said.	☐	☐	☐

Before the exam: practise speaking in small groups.
During the exam: if you don't understand a question, ask the examiner to repeat it.

2 **Prepare for Part One of the Speaking Test. Complete the first column of the table with your personal information. Then add one extra comment for each thing, as in the example.**

	personal information	extra comment
your name	Phyllis Smith	It's difficult to spell.
your city and country	Rotterdam	It's a nice place to live.
your name		
your city and country		
your family		
your home		
your job		
your studies		
your hobbies		

Speaking Test: Part One

3 You are going to listen to a recording of Part One of the Speaking Test. Before you listen, look at the questions that the examiner asks the male candidate in the photo at the bottom of the page. Which of the topics in exercise 2 does she ask him about?

- And what's your name?
- Joao, do you work or study in Portugal?
- And what about you, Joao? Do you like your work?
- And you Joao, do you have any hobbies?
- Do you think it's better to live in a small town or a big city?

4 4.8 Now listen to the recording. Does the examiner ask the questions in the same order as in exercise 3?

5 The transcript of the recording is on page 135. Read the transcript and underline the questions that the examiner asks the female candidate in the photo.

6 Work in groups of three and read the conversation out loud.

7 Work in groups of three and have similar conversations. Take turns to be the examiner and the candidates. Include the topics in exercise 2. Don't forget to agree/disagree with your partner and to express your preferences.

5.1 Career choices

READING

Escaping the rat race

Language Tip

The *rat race* refers to a working life where people compete hard for power and money, and don't have time to enjoy themselves.

1 Work in pairs. List the major changes that occur in a person's family life and working life. Tell your partner about a change you have experienced.

2 Look at the photographs in the magazine article below about people who have escaped the rat race. Do the pictures show them before or after their 'escape'?

3 Read the article and complete the table.

	In the past	In the present
Peter Van Der Groot	He worked in _____. ⟶	_____
Rob & Manda Brent	_____ ⟶	They live in _____.

TRUE LIFE STORIES

CHANGE YOUR LIFE

Does your 9 to 5 stress you out? Have you ever thought of escaping the rat race and doing something completely different? Well, here are some people who have done just that.

BACK TO THE LAND

In his early forties, Peter Van Der Groot was a successful stockbroker at the London Stock Exchange, with the typical rewards of success: a large beautiful home and a very healthy bank account. But Peter worked long hours, and he saw little of his home and family. He enjoyed his job, yes, but he was never there to see his children growing up. Then last year, the firm he worked for went bankrupt, and, unexpectedly, Peter had the opportunity to do something different.

So Peter and his family sold their house in London and moved to the countryside. They bought a smaller house with some land. Today, Peter is more relaxed. He spends time with his children, and he has seen them change into healthy, happy kids. He's started working on his land, growing fruit and vegetables. He still trades in shares, but only his own. He and his family have a modest, but comfortable life.

LIFE IN THE SUN

Husband and wife Rob and Manda Brent are teachers, but they've both resigned from their jobs, and neither of them plans to return to the school where they worked in Birmingham's city centre. Now they live in Italy, where they've bought a farmhouse in the Tuscan hills. 'We're going to offer bed and breakfast accommodation,' said Rob. 'We've never had our own business before, so it'll be quite a challenge. Plus we've borrowed a lot of money from the bank to get started.'

'In this first three-month period, we're settling in and reorganising the farmhouse,' said Manda. 'Then we'll open our doors to guests.'

Bed and breakfast will not be the only source of income, though. 'The farm has got olive trees and all the equipment for producing olive oil.'

It sounds as though Rob and Manda will be very busy. We wish them the best of luck!

4 Read the article again. Choose the best answer (A, B or C) for each question (1–5).

1 How old was Peter when he moved to the countryside?
   A 39   B 40   C between 41 and 45

2 Why did he move to the countryside?
   A because he wanted to work on his land
   B because he didn't like his job
   C because he wanted to spend more time with his family

3 What type of service are Rob and Manda going to provide?
   A rooms with breakfast and dinner
   B somewhere to sleep, and something to eat in the morning
   C rooms, but no meals

4 What business experience have they had?
   A three months of running a bed and breakfast
   B running a school in Birmingham
   C none

5 Where will their income come from?
   A from the selling of farm produce, and from paying guests
   B only from paying guests
   C only from the selling of farm produce

5 Read these comments and decide whether Peter or Rob said each one.

1 'I've started learning Italian. It really helps us make friends and business contacts.'
2 'My earnings have dropped, but my health has improved. I feel great!'
3 'I still deal in shares, but my wife deals with the family budget!'
4 'We haven't spent a lot on advertising, but people have already made enquiries.'
5 'We won't make a profit in the first year, but we hope to make money in the future.'

6 Work in pairs. Discuss the reasons for and against 'escaping the rat race'.

VOCABULARY

Money expressions

7 Match words from A and B to make expressions connected with money. You can use some words more than once.

A	B
1 borrow	a loss
2 earn	a profit
3 go	an income
4 make	bankrupt
5 spend	money
	over budget

8 Fill the gaps with expressions from exercise 7. Be careful with the verb forms!

0 My teenage children spend money more quickly than I can earn it!
1 Last year, I _____ _____ from the bank to buy my new car.
2 Sales decreased and they had lots of debts. In the end the company _____ _____.
3 She sold her old video games on eBay and _____ a huge _____.
4 The new Olympic stadium has already _____ _____ by 50 per cent.
5 People don't buy CDs now and small record shops are _____ a _____.
6 As a stockbroker, I _____ a healthy _____, but I wasn't happy.

The present perfect

We form the present perfect with *have/has* + the past participle of the verb.

They have (They've) resigned.

Past participles of regular verbs end with *-ed*: *talk – talked, hire – hired.*
For the past participle of irregular verbs, such as *speak – spoken, be – been, buy – bought*, you have to learn the forms.
Note that *go* uses two past participles in the present perfect.
He's gone to Rome. = He's in Rome now.
He's been to Rome. = He went to Rome and he came back.
We use the present perfect to talk about:

- something that has *recently* happened and that has a *consequence* or a visible result in the present.
  *I've just **bought** a new computer.*
- something that started in the past and continues in the present.
  *It's only 8.30 and I've already **answered** ten telephone calls this morning!*
- an action within a period of time which is not yet finished.
  *They **have been** colleagues since 2006.*

Note that we use the past simple to talk about a finished time and/or action.
I worked as a bank clerk from 2000 to 2005, then I left.

1 Look at the article on page 46 again. Underline all the verbs in the present perfect. How many are regular? How many are irregular?

2 Read about the changes in Petra Schein's life. Choose the correct options.

> **PETRA SCHEIN** (**1**) *has worked / worked* in human resources for Banque DeLux Online in Luxembourg since she left university. Four years ago, she (**2**) *has become / became* the HR manager of her branch when the former HR manager (**3**) *has retired / retired*. Last year, she (**4**) *has moved / moved* to the bank's head office. Since then, her responsibilities (**5**) *have increased / increased*. As a result, she has to spend more time at work.
>
> In her free time, Petra enjoys listening to music. She (**6**) *has wanted / wanted* to learn to play a musical instrument for a long time. Six months ago, she (**7**) *has bought / bought* a piano and this month she (**8**) *has started / started* taking lessons. But Petra doesn't have a lot of time to practise, so progress is slow.

3 Here are some time markers often used with the past simple (PS) or the present perfect (PP). Write PS or PP next to each one. Some can be used with both.

this week PP	last week _____	just _____	yesterday _____
today _____	... ever ... ? _____	when _____	since Friday _____
already _____	in 2007 _____	recently _____	three hours ago _____
not ... yet _____	for two days _____	never _____	How long ... ? _____

4 Put the time markers into the correct position in each sentence.

1 I have bought a guitar, but I don't know how to play it. (just)
2 Have you read any good books? (recently)
3 My friends want to go to the cinema, but I have seen the film. (already)
4 There's a great photography exhibition on in town. Have you seen it? (yet)
5 I've been here twenty minutes! Where have you been? (for)

5 Work in groups of three. Write five sentences about things you have or haven't done in your life. Include one false sentence. Read your sentences to the others. They try to identify the false sentence.

A: I've never eaten cheese.
B: I don't believe you. Haven't you ever eaten pizza?
A: Yes, but I take the cheese off.

LISTENING

Career changes

6 5.1 **Petra Schein and Alex Bélanger meet at a conference. Listen to their conversation. What are their jobs?**

Petra is a/an _____.
Alex was a/an _____; now he is a/an _____.

7 5.1 **Listen to the conversation again. Decide whether sentences 1–4 are 'Right' or 'Wrong'. If there is not enough information to choose 'Right' or 'Wrong', choose 'Doesn't say'.**

1 Petra and Alex have met before.
   A Right   B Wrong   C Doesn't say
2 Petra and Alex worked together three years ago.
   A Right   B Wrong   C Doesn't say
3 Alex takes pictures for magazines.
   A Right   B Wrong   C Doesn't say
4 Petra has moved to a different company.
   A Right   B Wrong   C Doesn't say

8 How has Alex's life changed in the last three years?

5.2 Achievements and plans

READING

In-company communications

1 **Read this email and answer the following questions.**

- Who is it to?
- Who is it from?
- What is the relationship between them?

From: Andres Martino
To: Elena Gonzalez
Subject: New cover designs
Date: 3 October

Hi Elena,

I'm off to the Book Fair this afternoon, but I see that the new designs haven't arrived yet.
Please can you:
– call the design office; ask them to send you the three designs for the book covers – this is <u>urgent</u>;
– write an email to the printers (Synapse) asking for price quotations for the three designs, in full colour, and in black and white;
– send the three designs to the printers.
Can you email me a full progress report by 6pm, please.
Andres

Learning Tip

Read your writing twice to check for spelling, punctuation and grammar mistakes.

2 **Read the email again and complete Elena's notes.**

THINGS TO DO TODAY
1 call _____ and ask for _____
2 write to _____ and get _____
3 send _____

3 **Work in pairs.**

Student A: You are Elena Gonzalez. Refer to your notes in exercise 2. Then phone Octavio Flores, head of the design office.
Student B: Go to page 128.

WRITING

Progress reports

Exam Success

In Part One of the Writing Test, you have to include the information given in bullet points, and sometimes invent your own details. Check that you include all the relevant information.

4 **Complete Elena's email to the printers.**

From: _____ **To:** _____ **Date:** _____
Subject: Price quotation
Could you _____?
I attach _____ and tomorrow
_____
Looking forward to _____
_____

5 **Write Elena's progress report to Andres. Write 30–40 words. Tell him:**

- what you have done
- what you haven't done and why
- future actions.

50

Talking about results

6 Work in pairs. Read this conversation between Berndt Reinhardt, the CEO of a publisher based in Cologne, Germany and an ex-colleague, Franka. Fill each gap with the present perfect form of a suitable verb.

Franka   Hello. It's nice to see you again. You're looking well.

Berndt   Thanks! I am well. I (**0**) 've just come (just) back from the Turin Book Fair.

Franka   Ah! One of your favourite events. How did it go?

Berndt   Oh, the fair was quite a success. We had a lot of interest in a new series of science titles that we (**1**) _____. And I met up with some old friends. Do you remember Nuno, from Lisbon? Yes, all in all, it was very pleasant. And I do enjoy Italian food.

Franka   It's delicious, isn't it? Well then, Berndt, has this been a good year for you?

Berndt   Yes, it has. We (**2**) _____ really well in Western Europe – we (**3**) _____ more books than ever before. And we (**4**) _____ distributing in countries in Eastern Europe as well – for example, in Poland and Hungary. Poland is doing very well. The demand for our books (**5**) _____ almost as high as in Spain and Portugal.

Franka   That's great! I can see you (**6**) _____ very busy.

Berndt   Well, of course! You know me.

Franka   So what's next then? I'm sure you've got something new planned.

Berndt   Well, we're going to move the actual printing to Slovakia. We have a new contract with a printing company in Bratislava. They're going to take over about 80 per cent of our book printing next year. It's going to cut our costs considerably, I hope.

Franka   What a coincidence! I (**7**) _____ (just) to Bratislava.

Berndt   Well, I'm going to be there next month. I'm going to discuss the contract with the printers. And after that, I think I'm going to take a few days' holiday. It's been a very busy year.

7 🔘 5.2 Listen to the conversation and check your answers.

8 Use information from the conversation in exercise 6 to complete this news item in the magazine *Publishing Weekly*.

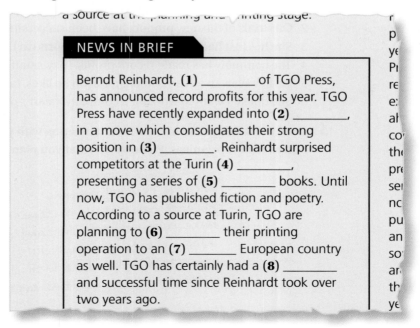

a source at the planning and printing stage.

NEWS IN BRIEF

Berndt Reinhardt, (**1**) _____ of TGO Press, has announced record profits for this year. TGO Press have recently expanded into (**2**) _____, in a move which consolidates their strong position in (**3**) _____. Reinhardt surprised competitors at the Turin (**4**) _____, presenting a series of (**5**) _____ books. Until now, TGO has published fiction and poetry. According to a source at Turin, TGO are planning to (**6**) _____ their printing operation to an (**7**) _____ European country as well. TGO has certainly had a (**8**) _____ and successful time since Reinhardt took over two years ago.

going to

We use *going to* + infinitive to express future plans and intentions:

We can use *going to* + infinitive with or without a time expression.
*We're not **going to** use that company again. They are very expensive.*
*She's **going to** look for a new job in the summer.*

> **I'm going to** take a holiday soon.

1 **Complete the dialogue with the correct form of the verbs in brackets.**

A Have you seen the news? The company (**1**) _____ (go / move) out of the city centre to a new site.

B I know, they (**2**) _____ (go / build) a new office block in the business park.

A That (**3**) _____ (go / be) difficult for a lot of people to get to.

B Yes, and the building (**4**) _____ (not / go / be) as big as this one.

A What do you mean? (**5**) _____ (they / go / fire) people?

B I don't know. I've heard that they (**6**) _____ (go / offer) good redundancy packages.

A Really? What (**7**) _____ (you / go / do)?
(**8**) _____ (you / go / apply for) redundancy?

B Why not? I've been here for 15 years. I could get quite a lot of money.

A Oh …

2 **Write sentences with *going to* using the prompts in brackets.**

0 Our offices are too small. (look for / new office building)
We're going to look for a new office building.

1 His company is in financial difficulties. (look for / new job)

2 Our trials of the new product have been successful. (launch / in summer)

3 She has just had a pay increase. (buy / sports car)

4 The company has made record profits. (pay / staff / bonus)

5 He has seen an advertisement for a job he likes. (apply for / job)

6 She doesn't want to work for a company. (start / own business)

3 **Read the notes you made at a recent meeting with your manager to discuss moving offices to new premises. Write down what you plan to do for each point.**

> arrange removal company
> arrange new details on company stationery
> make sure we keep the same phone numbers!
> inform clients and suppliers
> keep staff up-to-date with plans
> arrange for new utilities contracts

Negotiating a bank loan

4 🎧 5.3 Jack and Jill Hopkins have applied for a bank loan to start a new business. Listen to the meeting between Jack and the bank manager, and choose the best answer (A, B or C) for each question (1–6).

1 What kind of business are Jack and Jill going to start?
  A making ice creams
  B selling fruit and vegetables
  C making fruit drinks
2 How many flavours have they got at the moment?
  A one: strawberry
  B two: strawberry and pear
  C three: pear, banana and mango
3 Why do they want a loan?
  A to make more flavours and increase the amount they make
  B to experiment with new flavours
  C to take on more staff to meet demand
4 Where are they going to sell their products?
  A in their own shops
  B in snack bars and similar outlets
  C in bars and restaurants
5 What are they going to change about the way they work?
  A They plan to change the bottles they use.
  B They are going to use a different production process.
  C They aren't going to change anything.
6 Who are they going to market their products to?
  A young families with children
  B young people
  C health clubs

5 🎧 5.3 Listen again and complete the bank manager's questions.

1 Have you already started making and _____ your _____?
2 Are you going to _____ your range?
3 How do you plan to _____ the _____?
4 Who do you think is going to be your main _____?

6 Work in groups of four, in two pairs.

Pair A: Prepare questions a bank might ask before lending money. Use the questions in the Useful language box below and from exercise 5 to help you.
Pair B: Prepare ideas for a new business you want to start.

7 In your group of four, form two new pairs and act out the conversation.

Student A: You are the bank manager. Ask the questions you prepared in exercise 6.
Student B: You are the customer. Explain why you want to borrow money and answer the questions your partner asks. What is the bank manager's decision?

Useful language	
What do you do?	Have you ever borrowed money before?
Why do you want a loan?	Do you have any debts?
How much do you earn?	Do you have a credit card?
Do you have any other income?	How long have you been in business?

5.3

Reading Test: Parts One to Three

EXAM FORMAT

The Reading Test contains seven parts, with a total of 45 questions. There is a table on page 15 which summarises the types of question in each part.

l **Here is a question from Part One of the Reading Test. Work through the following steps with a partner.**

1 Read the text. Read the three options.
2 Which word in the text means the same as *sent*?
3 What does *on receipt of* mean?
4 Which comes first, the payment or the sending?
5 Which is the correct answer?

PART ONE

In each question, which sentence (**A**, **B** or **C**) is correct?

1 Goods will be dispatched on receipt of payment.
Customers must pay

A when they receive the goods.
B when the goods are sent.
C before the goods are sent.

EXAM PRACTICE

2 **Answer these questions from Part Two of the Reading Test.**

PART TWO

• Look at the list below. It shows items from a directory of business services.
• For questions **1–5**, decide which service (**A–H**) is suitable for each person.
• Do not use any letter more than once.

Business services
A Market research
B Displays, signs & posters
C Business finance
D Business trips & travel
E Internet design
F Office equipment
G Printing
H Shipping

1 Joan Marchaud wants to increase the visibility of her shop window.
2 Mikhail Romanov needs to send 12 prefabricated huts from his factory in Minsk to Riyadh.
3 Brian Ng is thinking of producing a new website for his pharmaceutical company.
4 Henrietta Obidike wants to sell her products in Europe, but she doesn't know if there is any demand.
5 Marie Fayet has to organise a flight to Brussels for her managing director.

---

3 Look at the chart from Part Three of the Reading Test below. Complete the text about sales in the Americas with the words from the box.

rise   dramatic   considerable   same   rose   slight

Sales in the Americas began at $11 million and (**1**) _____ in the first year. They continued to (**2**) _____ in the second year, and there was another increase in year 3. Then, there was a (**3**) _____ fall the following year. The next year, the level of sales stayed the (**4**) _____. Then, there was a (**5**) _____ increase in sales. The period ended with a (**6**) _____ drop.

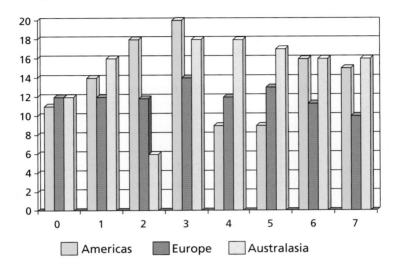

☐ Americas   ■ Europe   ☐ Australasia

4 Look at the chart from Part Three of the Reading Test again. Read this description. Is it about sales in Europe or Australasia? How much of the text do you need to read before you know the answer?

In this region, sales started at $12 million. The following year, they remained stable, and then fell slightly the next year. In year 3, there was an increase, but there was another fall the following year. Year 5 saw a slight rise, but then there was another fall. The period ended with sales falling slightly.

5 Answer these questions from Part Three of the Reading Test.

PART THREE
• This chart shows the sales of an electronics manufacturer over a seven-year period.
• Look at how the sales in the three regions changed over the seven years.
• Which year does each of the following statements (**1–5**) describe?
1 In the Americas, sales continued to increase, while there was a small fall in Europe.
2 This year, sales in Europe fell back to the level of the first two years.
3 After the previous year's disastrous fall, sales in Australasia reached their highest level over the seven-year period.
4 Sales stayed at the same level in Europe, but increased in both of the other two regions.
5 Sales in the Americas and in Europe fell slightly, but in Australasia they stayed at the same level as the previous year.

6.1

Business travel

Flight problems

1 Look at the words in the box. Underline the words for people and circle the words for documents.

> aircraft   check in   delay   journey   land   luggage   <u>passenger</u>   (passport)
> pilot   take off   travel   trip   air traffic controller   baggage handler
> boarding pass   business/economy/first class   flight attendant   identity card
> return/single ticket

2 Write the correct word from exercise 1 in each space.

1   How long does the _____ from here to Paris take?
2   Do you often _____ in your job?
3   'Have a good _____ !'
4   I'm coming back next week, so I need a _____ ticket.
5   You can only take one piece of _____ on the aeroplane.

3 🎧 6.1 Listen to four air passengers talking about their experiences. Complete the descriptions with the number of the speaker (1–4).

- Passenger _____ was very satisfied with the service he/she received.
- Passenger _____ missed his/her flight because of overbooking/lateness.
- Passenger _____ was delayed because of a strike.
- Passenger _____ was delayed because of bad weather.

4 🎧 6.1 Listen to the passengers again. Choose the best ending (A, B or C) for each sentence (1–4).

1   Passenger 1 was travelling
  A   alone.
  B   with one other person.
  C   with two other people.
2   Passenger 2 received instructions
  A   to wait in his hotel.
  B   to wait in the airport.
  C   to wait at the information desk.
3   Passenger 3 is
  A   disabled.
  B   hungry.
  C   famous.
4   According to Passenger 4, strikes
  A   are not common.
  B   occur regularly.
  C   are very rare.

5 Work in pairs. Tell your partner about your worst flying experience.

Reported speech

6 Look at these sentences. The first sentence in each pair is from the recording and is in reported speech. Complete the second sentence with direct speech (the words of the speakers).

1 The man at the desk said that the plane *was* already full.
  The man at the desk said, 'The plane _____ already full.'

2 The woman told me *to go* back to my hotel and *wait*.
  The woman said, '_____ back to your hotel and _____.'

3 She said they *were going* to close the airport, and she *didn't know* for how long.
  She said, 'We _____ to close the airport. I _____ for how long.'

4 The woman in the lounge said she *would bring* me some food.
  The woman in the lounge said, 'I _____ you some food.'

5 The announcement said there *would be* no cancellations that day, only delays.
  The announcement said, 'There _____ no cancellations today, only delays.'

7 When we report what people say, we usually change the verb tense. Complete the examples for reported speech in the table.

Direct speech		Reported speech	
tense	**example**	**tense**	**She said ...**
am/is/are	'It is late.'	*was/were*	it was late.
Present simple	'It leaves at 6am.'	Past simple	_____
Present continuous	'It is landing.'	Past continuous	_____
Past simple	'It arrived.'	Past perfect	it had arrived.
Present perfect	'It has taken off.'	Past perfect	_____
Future with *will*	'It will be early.'	*would*	_____
can	'It can leave.'	*could*	_____

Other modal verbs, such as *might, could, would* and *should*, do not change:
'*It could be delayed.*' → She said it **could** be delayed.

The past simple often stays the same:
'*The flight left on time.*' → She said the flight **left** on time.
Pronouns, possessive adjectives and some time expressions also change.

8 Underline any changes to pronouns, possessive adjectives and time expressions in the sentences in exercise 6.

9 Change these sentences into reported speech.

1 The flight attendant said, 'Your luggage is over the limit.'
  The flight attendant said (that) my _____

2 He said, 'You will have to pay an excess charge of £45.'
  He said (that) I _____

3 The flight attendant told us, 'The weather could be bad.'
  The flight attendant told them (that) the weather _____

4 She said, 'Your plane is going to take off at 15.55.'
  She said (that) my plane _____

5 The passenger said, 'I don't eat meat.'
  The passenger said (that) he _____

6 He said, 'I would like the vegetarian menu, please.'
  He said (that) he _____

No card, no ticket

1 Read this letter to the consumer help section of an in-flight magazine. Has anything similar ever happened to you or to anyone you know?

Dear *Editor*

Last month I bought a ticket online for a flight from Frankfurt to Lisbon. When I arrived at the airport, the person at the check-in desk wanted to see the credit card that I had used to purchase the ticket. I explained that somebody had stolen my card while I was in Germany, so I had a new one. This card had my name on it, but it had a different card number.

I showed the airline representative both my passport and my copy of the confirmation email. However, he shook his head and said I would have to purchase another ticket if I could not show him the original credit card.

Reluctantly, I paid €375 for another ticket to Lisbon. When I was back in Portugal, I contacted the airline customer service by phone and, after half an hour of conversation and argument, the airline company basically said there was nothing they could do. I don't think I should pay twice for my airline ticket. Can you help me?

Sean Bennet, *Lisbon*

2 Read the letter again. Decide whether these sentences are 'Right' or 'Wrong'. If there is not enough information to choose 'Right' or 'Wrong', choose 'Doesn't say'.

1 The passenger had purchased his ticket using his credit card.
  A Right   B Wrong   C Doesn't say
2 His flight was with a German airline.
  A Right   B Wrong   C Doesn't say
3 The names on the two cards were not the same.
  A Right   B Wrong   C Doesn't say
4 The passenger had paid less than €375 for his original ticket.
  A Right   B Wrong   C Doesn't say
5 He had to buy another ticket because he didn't have a credit card.
  A Right   B Wrong   C Doesn't say
6 The phone call to the airline customer service solved the problem.
  A Right   B Wrong   C Doesn't say

3 Compare your answers with a partner. For the questions that you have answered 'Right' or 'Wrong', which words helped you to decide the answer? For the questions you answered 'Doesn't say', why did you give this answer?

4 Work in pairs. Discuss what the magazine editor could do to help Mr Bennet.

5 This is the editor's reply. The paragraphs are in the wrong order. Put them into the correct order (1–5).

Dear *Traveller*

- ☐ I hope that we have been of help to you and that your next trip is trouble-free.

- ☐ The terms and conditions on the airline's website say that, for security reasons, to obtain a boarding pass, you must present the same credit card that you used to buy your ticket.

- ☐ The next time you have a problem like this, ask to talk to a manager or a supervisor. Remember, a check-in clerk's job is to apply the rules. A manager can decide to make an exception. I recommend that you contact the airline again, explain your circumstances, and ask for a refund.

- ☐ Dear Sean,
Thank you for writing to us about your experience. I agree with you that it seems unfair of the airline to charge you for another ticket, but the airline rules tell a different story.

- ☐ This is because the airline wants to prevent someone from buying a ticket with a stolen card. This is reasonable, but it is easy to check new cards with a simple phone call. Charging you another €375 was unreasonable.

6 Check your answers.

1 Paragraph 1 introduces the reason for writing.
2 Paragraph 2 gives factual information about the situation
3 Paragraph 3 explains the reason for the situation.
4 Paragraph 4 gives additional information and advice.
5 Paragraph 5 makes a concluding comment.

7 You are the customer services manager of the airline. Write a follow-up letter (60–80 words) to Mr Bennet telling him the following. Write five paragraphs as in exercise 6.

- The editor of the in-flight magazine contacted the airline about the complaint.
- The check-in staff have explained the details of the situation.
- The airline tries to protect its customers from credit card fraud.
- On this occasion, they are happy to give him a refund.
- They hope he will use the airline again.

6.2 Travel arrangements

Hotel amenities

1 Work in pairs. Here are some amenities you can find in a hotel. Which things do you think are most useful when travelling? Why?

a lift	free newspapers	a direct-dial telephone
a jacuzzi	a swimming pool	room service
a mini bar	air conditioning	an Internet connection
a hair dryer	a conference room	conference equipment
a fitness room	translation services	laundry service

2 You are looking for a hotel to host your company's European sales conference. Read this hotel brochure. Underline all the amenities the hotel provides. Is this a suitable hotel for the conference?

The Carlton is one of the world's finest luxury hotels. It features individually designed rooms, including master and junior suites, with private balconies that offer beautiful views over the gardens and the sea. All rooms are equipped to the highest standards.

Excellent, contemporary cuisine and an extensive wine list are the main features at the Carlton Restaurant. The restaurant places great emphasis on the finest local, seasonal ingredients to produce a modern, healthy menu. Explore the gardens and stroll through the grounds to the beach and sea. Spend time in the state-of-the-art gym, indoor and outdoor swimming pools, tennis courts, and on the nine-hole golf course.

Our business centre meets the needs of our business guests. It provides secretarial and translation services, and business support – from computers, printers and scanners to high-speed Internet access, photocopying and faxing facilities. In addition, we offer a 24-hour multilingual concierge service, airline reservations, Internet broadband access, a complimentary newspaper and direct-dial multi-line telephones with voice mail.

Booking enquiries

3 You decide to contact the hotel for more information. Read the email to Paul Rogers, the hotel bookings manager, and correct the five mistakes.

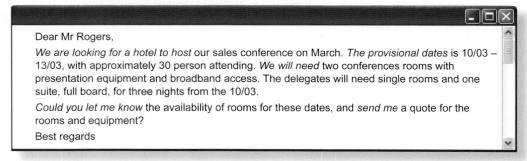

Dear Mr Rogers,

We are looking for a hotel to host our sales conference on March. *The provisional dates* is 10/03 – 13/03, with approximately 30 person attending. *We will need* two conferences rooms with presentation equipment and broadband access. The delegates will need single rooms and one suite, full board, for three nights from the 10/03.

Could you let me know the availability of rooms for these dates, and *send me* a quote for the rooms and equipment?

Best regards

4 Write a new email to the Carlton Hotel to make a booking enquiry. Use the phrases in italics, but invent your own details. Write 60–80 words.

5 Read the booking enquiry email from your partner. Write a reply confirming the availability of the rooms and equipment, and giving the prices. Write 60–80 words.

At the hotel

6 **Use the prompts to write full sentences about what these hotel employees do.**

0   A receptionist / answer / telephone / deal / guests
    A receptionist answers the telephone and deals with guests.
1   A business centre secretary / deal / business people's / needs
2   A porter / carry / people's / bags / suitcases
3   A waiter / work / restaurant / bring / food / customers
4   A chambermaid / clean / tidy / hotel bedrooms

7 **Look at the sentences. Which member of staff said what? Choose from the jobs in exercise 6.**

1   'Good afternoon. Carlton Hotel. How may I help you?'
2   'Can I help you with your luggage, Madam?'
3   'May I clean your room now?'
4   'Are you ready to order, Sir?'
5   'I'll call the technician, Madam.'

8 **Match sentences 1–5 in exercise 7 with sentences A–E.**

A   'No, I just can't decide.'
B   'Yes, please. I've got some very heavy suitcases.'
C   'Yes, hello. I'm phoning to check if my online booking went through.'
D   'Thank you. And ask him to come immediately!'
E   'Yes, of course. I'm just going out.'

9 🔘 6.2 **Listen to five conversations and check your answers to exercise 8.**

10 🔘 6.2 **Listen to the conversations again and choose the best answer (A, B or C) for each question (1–5).**

1   When does the caller want to stay in the hotel?
    A   on Tuesday 14
    B   on Tuesday 23
    C   on Thursday 23
2   Which luggage does the woman need help with?
    A   the three suitcases on the right
    B   the two large suitcases on the left
    C   the three suitcases on the left
3   When will the guest's trousers be ready?
    A   today, at 8pm
    B   tomorrow, at 8am
    C   tomorrow, at 8pm
4   What does the guest choose?
    A   the dish of the day
    B   fish and vegetables
    C   meat and vegetables
5   What is the speaker's problem?
    A   She can't connect her laptop to the video projector.
    B   She can't connect up to the Internet.
    C   The Internet connection is slow.

11 **The transcript of the recording is on page 137. Work in pairs and read the conversations out loud. Then practise your own conversations using the words in exercises 7 and 8.**

Arranging business travel

1 How do you say these times? Compare with a partner. How many different ways can you say the times?

A 09.00   B 12.15   C 07.45   D 21.30   E 17.05   F 22.40

2 🎧 6.3 Listen to the announcements and write the times.

Announcement 1	the next train from platform 6 departs at	_____
Announcement 2	the Glasgow to London coach is at	_____
Announcement 3	the Bristol Express will arrive at	_____
Announcement 4	there are no flights until	_____

3 Michael Burnett has asked his secretary to book a flight from London Heathrow Airport to Paris Charles De Gaulle Airport. Read his note and look at the flight times. In pairs, decide which flights Michael could take.

Have to be in Paris, Wed, meeting at 10am. Please book flight, LH – CDG, one way. (Remember, airport – Paris office takes about an hour.) Thanks.

Michael

DAILY FLIGHTS
FROM: LONDON HEATHROW AIRPORT
TO: PARIS CHARLES DE GAULLE AIRPORT

Air France		British Midland		British Airways	
LHR	CDG	LHR	CDG	LHR	CDG
06:40	09:00	06:35	09:10	06:20	08:25
09:15	11:25	10:40	12:55	07:20	09:40
13:05	15:15	13.10	15:25	11:40	13:55
18:00	20:10	16:00	18:15	17:10	19:25
20:15	22:25	19:00	21:10	19:40	21:55

4 🎧 6.4 Listen to Michael's secretary calling the travel agent. Which flight does she book?

Flight No. _____   Time _____

5 Complete the sentences with the words in the box.

available   book   booking   booking   fully booked   passenger's

1 I'd like to _____ a flight to Paris.
2 I'm afraid the flight is _____.
3 Is there a seat still _____?
4 Would you like to make a _____?
5 Can I have the _____ name, please?
6 The _____ is for one passenger.

6 🎧 6.4 Listen to the conversation again and check your answers.

Learning Tip

Improve your speaking by recording yourself and listening to the recording. What do you need to improve most – pronunciation, intonation or general fluency?

Making a booking

7 Work in pairs. Practise making flight bookings using the information below.

Student A (passenger): You want to book a flight.
Phone the travel agent.

- Ask to book a flight from London to Paris.
- Your meeting is at 2pm.
- You want to arrive before the meeting but not too early.
- Remember to allow one hour to travel from the airport to the office.
- Write down the flight number and time.

Student B (travel agent): Someone calls to book a flight to Paris from London.
Use the timetable in exercise 3.

- Take the name of the passenger.
- Some of the flights are already fully booked.
- At the end, give the person the flight number and time.

Changes to flight details

8 Complete the email from a travel agent to business clients using the information below. Write 60–80 words. Give the email to your partner.

- Flights to Paris next week will be diverted to Lyons because of an air traffic control dispute.
- You do not know how long the dispute will last.
- Offer a refund or a booking for a later date.

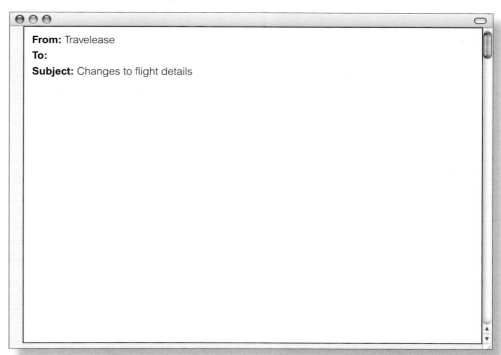

From: Travelease
To:
Subject: Changes to flight details

9 Reply to the travel agent's email stating what action you want them to take. Give the email to your partner. Will you take the action your client wants you to take?

6.3

Writing Test: Part One

In Part One of the Writing Test, you have to write to a colleague within your company. Sometimes it may be necessary to use a formal style of writing; in other cases your message can be more informal. This depends on who you are writing to and why.

1 Look at the email and message below. Who are they from? Who are they to? What are they about?

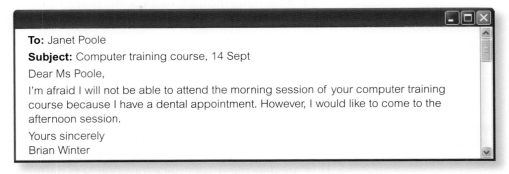

To: Janet Poole
Subject: Computer training course, 14 Sept
Dear Ms Poole,
I'm afraid I will not be able to attend the morning session of your computer training course because I have a dental appointment. However, I would like to come to the afternoon session.
Yours sincerely
Brian Winter

Hi Hector,
While I'm away, can you contact the technician? My printer still isn't working properly, and I'll need it when I come back from Portugal. See you in ten days. Bye.
Rachel

2 Both of the messages contain a request. Underline each request.

3 Which message is formal? Which is informal?

4 Read the instructions from Part One of the Writing Test and the note. The note is too long. Rewrite the note using 30–40 words.

PART ONE
- You have to write a report for a client, but your colleague has not sent you his data yet.
- Write a **note** to your colleague:
  - telling him that he is late
  - reminding him of why you need the data
  - giving him a date by which he must send his data.
- **Write 30–40 words.**

Dear Gianni,
I'm writing to tell you that you haven't sent me your data yet, and you're late. Please remember that I need your data because I have to write a report. The report is for the company Cairoli & Sons. Cairoli & Sons are a very important client for us, so I don't want to be late. Please send me your data for the report for Cairoli & Sons by tomorrow morning, otherwise I won't be able to write the report in time.
Thank you very much.
Margaretha

5 Look at these three items of internal communication. They use three different styles: formal, neutral and informal. Which is which?

MEMO		
	To:	All members of staff
	From:	Arnel Ranjit – quality control
	Date:	3 May
		Next week, there will be a visit from the ISO inspectors for this year's quality inspection. Everyone please be as helpful as possible to ensure that we obtain certification again this year.

To: Human resources manager
Subject: Request for transfer
Dear Mrs Odell,
I would like to request a transfer to the Oxford branch. My wife has just changed her job, and as a result, we will have to move to the Oxford area.
Yours sincerely,
James McGuire

Hi Toni,

Can you email the new designs to me again? The files don't open on my computer, and I need to make a few alterations before I send them on to the printers. Thanks.

Pat

6 Underline the words and phrases in the formal and informal messages that helped you to decide.

7 Answer the exam question. Use the phrases below to help you.

EXAM PRACTICE

Exam Success

Leave enough time to check:
• your writing for spelling, grammar and punctuation mistakes.
• that you have included all the relevant information.
• the number of words.

PART ONE
• One of your staff has sent you a project report.
• Write an **email** to:
  • thank her for the report
  • congratulate her on her work
  • arrange a meeting to discuss her conclusions.
• **Write 30–40 words.**

Phrases for starting a short communication	Phrases for ending a short communication
Dear Ms/Mr_____ (formal/neutral)	Yours faithfully (formal)
Dear _____ (*first name*) (informal)	Yours sincerely (formal)
Hi _____ (*first name*) (informal)	Kind regards (formal/neutral)
	Best regards (formal/neutral)
	Best wishes (neutral/informal)
	Bye (informal)

7.1

Products and services

READING

I   Work in pairs. Read the customer testimonials from a product brochure. Then read the brochure and decide which features the two customers are referring to.

> **BILL TALIBOV, Illinois:** 'At last! A way to keep my house plants alive and looking beautiful!'
>
> **LYNNE NAPOLEON, Cardiff:** 'It's great to have a system that knows what I like and does those things for me!'

SMART HOMES: THE FUTURE IS HERE

These days, most houses have appliances that contain some level of remote control. In the future, with our unique *ResidentIntel domotics* system, you can extend this remote control to all parts of your home. With the *ResidentIntel* system installed, your home could contain several computers, some built into the walls, enabling you, the homeowner, to control applications in one room, from any other room in the house. *ResidentIntel* makes your home life easier and more convenient.

PERSONALISED SPACES

Our system can actually recognise the person who enters the room, and adjust the heating and lighting settings to that person's personal preferences. It can even turn on your favourite music. You simply wear a badge so that the system can identify you. Our more sophisticated systems can identify you from your movements, body temperature and other characteristics.

MONEY-SAVING INTELLIGENCE

ResidentIntel takes advantage of cheaper, non-peak electricity rates, and gives choices for comfort, safety and energy conservation. Our system is the most advanced on the market and guarantees you savings.

HOME SECURITY

When you are away, on holiday, for example, our system can switch lights on and off, making the house look occupied to potential burglars. And when there is an emergency, the system can call the police or fire brigade.

TOTAL CONTROL

And you can even control the system when you are out of the house. Just call using your cell phone or an ordinary phone, and you'll be able to communicate with your house: make it warmer for your arrival home, turn the oven on or start the DVD recorder. It's the easiest way to feel in control.

GREEN GARDEN

ResidentIntel can control watering systems for your garden and indoor plants so that they will receive water only when they need it. Your garden will be the most attractive in your street, even when you are away on holiday.

2   Choose the best ending (A, B or C) for each sentence (1–3).

1   In the future, homes could
    A   require more maintenance by the homeowner.
    B   have a higher level of remote control.
    C   be very expensive.

2   One advantage of the system is that
    A   it can be controlled from anywhere in the house.
    B   it switches off when you are on holiday.
    C   your telephone bills will be cheaper.

3   The system can
    A   calculate your electricity bill.
    B   recognise a person from the way he/she moves.
    C   call you on your cell phone.

Comparatives and superlatives

We use the comparative form to compare an object with another or other similar objects:

*The PC is **more expensive** than the printer. The fax machine is **less expensive** than the printer.*

We use the superlative form to compare an object with the whole group:

*The laptop is **the most expensive** item. The fax machine is **the least expensive** item.*

We also use *as* + adjective + *as*:

*The PC isn't **as expensive as** the laptop.*

We can use the comparative form to show that something is changing.

*These systems are becoming **cheaper and cheaper**.*

3 Look at the labels and notes. Decide whether the following statements are true or false.

1 A The Dell is more expensive than the Fujitsu Siemens. ☐
   B The Fujitsu Siemens is the most expensive computer. ☐
   C The LG is the least expensive computer. ☐

2 A Brite is cheaper than Kleeno. ☐
   B Brite isn't as cheap as San-It. ☐
   C San-It is the cheapest cleaning service. ☐

3 A Domesticus is the largest company. ☐
   B ResidentIntel is smaller than Autocasa. ☐
   C Autocasa isn't as big as ResidentIntel. ☐

Dell €562
LG €450
Fujitsu Siemens €805

Brite cleaning service: €750 per month

San-It cleaning service: €600 per month

Kleeno cleaning service: €750 per month

ResidentIntel: 23 branches, 6 countries

AutoCasa: 5 branches, 2 countries

Domesticus: 300 branches, 27 countries

4 Work in pairs. Write sentences comparing the items. Use the comparative form of the adjective or *as … as.*

0 Emails / faxes (efficient)
   Emails are more efficient than faxes.
1 a photocopier / a scanner (complicated)
2 a computer / a typewriter (modern)
3 a pen drive / a PDA (useful)
4 skype / a conference phone (cheap)
5 a laser printer / a photocopier (quick)

Hotels of the future

1 🔘 **7.1** Aisha Ghadir, of Hydro Palace Hotels, is giving an interview about a very unusual chain of hotels. Listen and decide what makes these hotels different.

2 🔘 **7.1** Listen to the interview again and complete the table.

Hotel	Anemone	Nautilus	Atlantis
Location	(1) _____	Fiji	Dubai
Opened	two years ago	(2) _____	going to open early next year
Depth (below sea level)	10 metres	14 metres	(5) _____ metres
Number of rooms	20	(3) _____	160
Nightly rate	$940	$1360	(6) $_____
Building costs	$47 million	(4) $_____ million	$520 million

3 Write five sentences comparing the hotels. Use the information in the table and the superlative form of these adjectives.

| exclusive | expensive | deep | large | new |

Customer service questionnaire

4 Complete this customer service questionnaire about the last hotel you stayed in. Then ask your partner the questions.

Customer Feedback HolidayHotel.net	You	Your partner
Name of client		
Name of hotel		
Where was the hotel? How many nights did you stay? How many people were in your party? Please rate the following things from 1 (unacceptable) to 5 (excellent): • comfort • cleanliness • food • bar • facilities • room service • personal attention • value for money Would you stay at the hotel again? Would you recommend this hotel?		

5 Write a paragraph summarising the differences and similarities in the experiences you and your partner had. Then read your partner's paragraph and underline the expressions of comparison. Have you given the same information?

6 Look at the following things you can consider when choosing a business school. Tick the five things that are most important to you. Compare with three other students and agree on the most important features.

academic reputation of the school	tuition fees
attractiveness of the school buildings	variety of subjects on the curriculum
business experience of the lecturers	percentage of graduates in work
preparation for a career in business	percentage of graduates earning over €100,000 per annum
proximity to home	percentage of graduates in executive positions
quality of the teaching	
timetable flexibility	

7 Read the text quickly and look at the chart. Which five features in exercise 6 are shown in the chart?

Choosing a business school

This year, the new students at Freidank's School of Business, in Bonn, (1) _____ that the most important characteristic when choosing a business school was career preparation. In fact, career preparation was the top-ranked characteristic for both new students and (2) _____ parents.

In contrast, last year, the new students put quality of the teaching as the (3) _____ important characteristic, and career preparation shared (4) _____ place with availability of subjects.

The new students this year gave more importance to the attractiveness of the campus (5) _____ the new students did

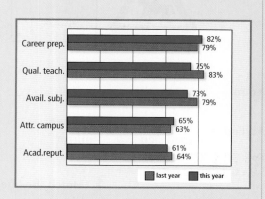

last year. It is interesting to note that the new students this year considered the school's academic reputation (6) _____ least important of the five characteristics, even (7) _____ important than an attractive campus. Last year, the new students (8) s the academic reputation was more important than an attractive campus.

8 Read the text again and choose the correct word (A, B or C) to fill each gap.

1 A said   B says   C saying
2 A their   B his   C its
3 A more   B most   C less
4 A first   B last   C second
5 A that   B which   C than
6 A a   B as   C the
7 A as   B less   C more
8 A think   B thought   C thinks

7.2 Orders and contracts

Shapes and sizes

1 What is your favourite possession? Describe it to your partner without saying its name. Can your partner guess?

2 Complete the table. Use the noun or adjective which is related to the word in *italics*.

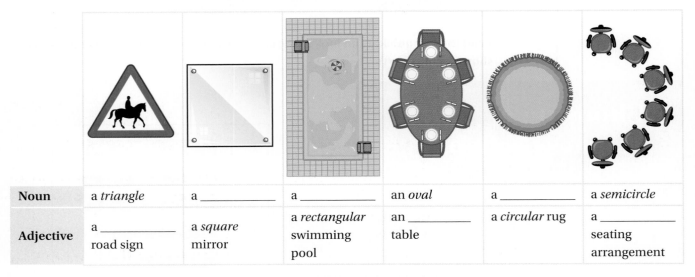

Noun	a *triangle*	a _____	a _____	an *oval*	a _____	a *semicircle*
Adjective	a _____ road sign	a *square* mirror	a *rectangular* swimming pool	an _____ table	a *circular* rug	a _____ seating arrangement

3 Match the questions (1–9) with the answers (A–J).

0 What's the length of an A4 sheet of paper?   A It's 17in (inches).
1 What's the width of that orange box?   B It's 2.5m deep.
2 What's the height of that lamp?   C It's £200.
3 What's the depth of that swimming pool?   D It's 29.7cm long.
4 What's the size of your LCD monitor?   E It's 13cm wide.
5 What's the weight of that leather briefcase?   F It's 2.5 kilos.
6 What's the price of that mobile phone?   G It's 50cm in diameter.
7 What's the diameter of the wheel?   H It's 1.8m high.
8 What colour is the screen?   I It's blue.
9 What is that desk made of?   J It's made of wood and metal.

4 Rewrite questions 1–7 in exercise 3 starting with *How*.

0 How long is an A4 sheet of paper?

1 _____
2 _____
3 _____
4 _____
5 _____
6 _____
7 _____

5 Work in groups of three.

Student A: Think of an object you use at work.

Students B and C: Ask questions to find out the object. You only have ten questions!

Making an order

6 🔘 7.2 **Listen to the telephone conversation between a caller and a sales assistant in an office furniture shop. Answer the questions.**

1 What does the customer want to buy? _____

2 What colour does he want? _____

3 Does he buy the item? _____

7 🔘 7.2 **Listen to the telephone conversation again and complete the missing information.**

Size of FC12W	Price
Height: (**1**) _____ cm Width: (**2**) _____ cm Depth: (**3**) _____ cm	FC12W: (**5**) £_____ FC12M: (**6**) £_____
Number of drawers	**Colours**
(**4**) _____	FC12W: (**7**) _____ wood finish FC12M: blue, (**8**) _____ or grey metal

8 **Work in pairs. Look at these questions from the telephone conversation and decide whether the customer (C) or the assistant (A) asked each question. Then use the questions and the information in the table in exercise 7 to practise the conversation.**

1 Good morning, Office Design. How can I help you? _____

2 And how high is your desk? _____

3 So you haven't got one in plastic? _____

4 How many drawers have they got? _____

5 How much do they cost? _____

6 And what colours do they come in? _____

9 **Work in pairs.**

Student A: Go to page 127.

Student B: You are going to organise a local public event and you would like to rent a children's inflatable toy. Look at the pictures below and call Inflatable World Ltd. (Student A) to ask for information about the size, weight and cost of the items.

Article Number	4832-CA (castle)
Size (metres)	Length: _____ Width: _____ Height: _____
Weight (kilograms)	_____
Prices (euros)	4-hour rental: _____ 8-hour rental: _____ 2-day rental: _____

Article Number	685–SL (slide)
Size (metres)	Length: _____ Width: _____ Height: _____
Weight (kilograms)	_____
Prices (euros)	4-hour rental: _____ 8-hour rental: _____ 2-day rental: _____

Service providers

1 Read the newspaper articles and fill the gaps with the words in the box.

contracts	provider	landlines	service users	broadband	technical support

70 per cent of Internet **(1)** _____ say they are not satisfied with their Internet service **(2)** _____ . The Consumer Protection Office received 24,210 complaints about telecommunications last year, of which 47 per cent related to the Internet, 36 per cent to mobile phones and the rest to **(3)** _____ .

An increasing number of Internet service providers are offering faster and faster **(4)** _____ connections for a monthly charge. But we have found that in reality some of these are no quicker than dial-up connections. In addition, **(5)** _____ is almost non-existent in many cases.

The Internet Users Association reports that the biggest problems are with cancelling **(6)** _____ .

2 You are going to find out if your classmates' experiences with Internet service providers (ISP) is similar or different to those reported in the news stories. Work in pairs to write a questionnaire. Use the ideas in the left column of the questionnaire to help you.

	Questions	Person 1	Person 2	Person 3	Person 4
name of Internet service provider (ISP)?	What is the name of your Internet service provider?				
broadband connection?	Do you have				
dial-up connection?					
technical support – opinion?					
monthly charge – opinion?					
overall opinion? (fast / easy to use / reliable / efficient / value for money)					

3 Ask several people the questions in your questionnaire. Then analyse the results of the questionnaire. Which company provides the best service? Report your conclusions to the class. Do you all agree?

Changing ISP

4 🔘 7.3 **Bryan Ross runs a small courier company. He currently pays between €100 and €200 each month for Internet and telephone services from NatNet. He is looking for a cheaper option. Listen to Bryan's telephone call to Maroon Communications and complete his notes.**

> <u>MaroonBusinessOne package</u>
>
> What do I get?
> - unlimited (1) _____
> - mobiles & (2) _____
> - 24-hour (3) _____
> - no charge for (4) _____
> - price of phone not included in package
>   number of mobile lines (5) _____
>   calls to technical support line (6) _____
>   guaranteed broadband (7) _____
>   broadband connection to (8) _____
>   How much?
> - first three months (9) _____
> - after that (10) _____
> - contract lasts (11) _____

5 **Compare your answers to exercise 4 with your partner. Do you think Bryan should change to the MaroonBusinessOne package? Why? / Why not?**

ISP contract

6 **Put the sentences in this email from NatNet into the correct order (1–5). What is the purpose of the email?**

> _____ We look forward to your custom in the future.
>
> _____ This request is now being processed.
>
> _____ The contract will be cancelled at the end of the current billing period.
>
> _____ You will be able to use your NatNet 24/7 until then.
>
> _____ We have received a request to cancel contract number 738387.

7 **Write an email from Maroon Communications to Bryan Ross to confirm his new contract with MaroonBusinessOne. Use the email in exercise 6 as a guide, and write about 40 words.**

7.3 Listening Test: Part Two

EXAM FORMAT

In Part Two of the Listening Test, you have to listen to a short telephone conversation or monologue that lasts about a minute and a half. There is a table on page 34 which summarises the types of question in each part.

APPROACH

- Before the telephone conversation starts, you will hear some instructions. Listen to the instructions and read the form.
- Understand what the conversation is about. Who is calling? (a man or a woman?)
- After the instructions, you have ten seconds before the conversation starts. Read each line in order to see what kind of information you need to listen for.
- As you listen to the conversation, write down the possible answers. Sometimes you will have more than one answer for each question.
- During the second listening, cross out the incorrect information.
- After listening twice, you will have ten seconds to check your answers.

1 Here is a typical task from Part Two of the Listening Test. Read the instructions. Predict what kind of information is needed for each question: what kinds of numbers or words will be heard? Do not listen to the recording at this stage.

PART TWO
- Look at the form below.
- Some information is missing.
- You will hear a man telephoning a training company.
- For each question (**1–7**), fill in the missing information in the numbered space using a **word**, **numbers** or **letters**.
- You will hear the conversation twice.

Course booking

Training course:	(1) .... skills
Course code:	(2) ....
Date:	(3) ....
Number of participants:	(4) ....
Name of company:	(5) .... Ltd
Contact name:	(6) Charles ....
Contact tel. number:	(7) 01536–...

2 7.4 **Listen to the conversation and write down the possible answers.**

3 7.4 **Listen again and cross out the incorrect information.**

Listening Test: Part Three

EXAM FORMAT

APPROACH

Exam Success

- Before you listen, read all the instructions and the questions very carefully.
- Check your answers are clearly marked in the pauses between listenings.
- Answer all the questions.

In Part Three of the Listening Test, you have to listen to a monologue that lasts about two minutes. There is a table on page 34 which summarises the types of question in each part.

- Follow the same approach as in Part Two of the Listening Test.
- Try to predict what kinds of words you need to listen for.
- Note that you have 20 seconds to check your answers.

4 🔘 7.5 **Here is a typical task from Part Three of the Listening Test. Read the instructions, but do not listen to the recording at this stage.**

- Look at the notes about a company.
- Some information is missing.
- You will hear a presentation by the company's managing director.
- For each question (**1–7**), fill in the missing information in the numbered space using one or two words.
- You will hear the presentation twice.

Platt & Sons Ltd

Products:	(1) ....
Original line of business:	(2) making ....
The first models were for:	(3) ....
Main customers today:	(4) ....
New product line available from:	(5) ....
Future plans: to export to the EU, first to:	(6) .... and Germany
Reports of financial difficulties are:	(7) ....

5 'Signal' words on the recording can help you identify the answers to the questions. These words can be synonyms (words with the same meaning), collocations (words that go together) or the actual words in the question. Work in pairs and match each group of 'signal' words below with the questions in the exam task above. Write the numbers.

Our customers now 4
We intend to _____
We manufacture _____
You might have seen _____

We expect to bring out our _____
He started off by producing _____
The machines made in 1958 _____

6 🔘 7.5 **Now listen to the recording and fill in the missing information in the exam task. Did you notice the 'signal' words?**

8.1 Manufacturing processes

READING

1 Work in pairs. Look at the photographs and decide which is 'before' and which is 'after'. Give reasons for your answer.

2 Read the newspaper article from *Weekend West* quickly to find the following:

1 the name of the company it talks about
2 what kind of products the company makes
3 who uses the company's products.

Graffiti a problem? Just wash it!

IT HAS BEEN described as art by some people, but to others it's an ugly and depressing aspect of modern life. What is it? Graffiti, of course. Look around your city today and you can see graffiti on buildings, walls, doors and even on buses or trains that have stayed in one place for too long. But where modern technology creates a problem, it also finds a solution. Last week, *Weekend West* was shown around the factory of a small but highly innovative and successful company, Hubdean.

Hubdean's achievement is a series of special paints which are graffiti-resistant. How do they work? It couldn't be simpler. Take any graffiti-covered surface. First, a treatment called Agproclear is applied. Then, using a very hot pressure jet, this treatment is removed and the graffiti disappears at the same time. Now you have a clean wall. But before this clean wall can be painted on by vandals, a new product, Agproshield, is applied. This paint has a special surface which gives it two important properties. Firstly, spray paint won't stick to the surface very well, and secondly, the whole surface can be cleaned very easily, just using water. Once the surface is painted, no specialist equipment is needed to keep the area clean and graffiti-free.

Not surprisingly, Hubdean's products are used by both local councils and private companies all over the UK, and now orders are being received from around the world. This presents the company with a problem, however. Can they increase production to satisfy the extra demand? Options include building a second factory, dedicated to the most popular products, or licensing a major international company to manufacture their products. The future is looking good for Hubdean!

3 Read the article again. Decide whether these sentences are 'Right' or 'Wrong'. If there is not enough information to choose 'Right' or 'Wrong', choose 'Doesn't say'.

1 Agproclear was developed by Hubdean.
  A Right   B Wrong   C Doesn't say
2 After painting a surface with Agproshield, you can wash it with water.
  A Right   B Wrong   C Doesn't say
3 Most of Hubdean's business comes from private companies.
  A Right   B Wrong   C Doesn't say
4 Hubdean has two factories in the UK.
  A Right   B Wrong   C Doesn't say
5 A large international company is going to buy Hubdean.
  A Right   B Wrong   C Doesn't say

The passive

The object of the active sentence becomes the subject of the passive sentence.

They apply Agproclear. (Agproclear = the object)
*Agproclear **is applied**.* (Agproclear = the subject)

Subject	*be*	Past participle
Agproclear	is	applied.
Orders	are being	received.
The wall	was	cleaned.
The graffiti	has been	removed.
The licence	is going to be	sold.
The area	will be	painted.
The surface	can be	washed.

We use the passive:
- to focus attention on what happens, not who does it.
  Weekend West **was shown** *around the factory.*
- to say how something is done.
  *The graffiti **is removed** from the walls.*

We can use *by* + 'agent' to say who or what does the action.
*Hubdean's products **are used** by local councils.*

4 Underline the passive forms in the newspaper article. Circle the subject in each sentence. Which sentences also give the agent?

5 Rewrite the second sentence in each pair in the passive. Decide whether the subject of the sentence is singular or plural and use the correct form of *be*.

0 The system carries out the quality checks automatically.
   The quality checks are carried out automatically.
1 If there's a delay, we inform the client.
   If there's a delay, the client _____.
2 He's testing the new system.
   The new system _____.
3 They showed us around the factory.
   We _____.
4 We have increased production.
   Production _____.
5 They will clean the area tomorrow.
   The area _____.

6 Read the testimonial from a customer of Hubdean. Choose the correct verb forms.

We (**1**) *manage / are managed* a number of community centres in the North of England. Until recently, we (**2**) *faced / are faced* a big problem with both vandals and graffiti. Our centres (**3**) *use / are used* every day, but because there is nobody on site during the night, the buildings (**4**) *were vandalising / were being vandalised* regularly. We (**5**) *tried / were tried* various products to get rid of the graffiti. But every time it (**6**) *cleaned / was cleaned* off, the walls (**7**) *defaced / were defaced* again almost immediately. Then we (**8**) *contacted / were contacted* Hubdean. Their consultants (**9**) *have worked / have been worked* closely with our maintenance staff and our buildings (**10**) *have protected / have been protected* from vandalism.

Supply and demand

1 Look at the words in the box. Tick the words that you already know and find the meaning of the others in a dictionary.

> automated   capacity   delivery   demand   handmade   order
> output   plant   produce   product   supply   warehouse

2 Choose the correct word in each sentence.

1 Hubdean need to build a new *plant / warehouse* to store their goods.
2 The company has received new *orders / deliveries* for their products from satisfied customers.
3 The existing factory cannot make enough to satisfy *supply / demand*.
4 The products are made using *an automated / a handmade* assembly line.
5 The factory is currently working at full *capacity / output*.
6 An international company could manufacture Hubdean's *produce / products* under licence.

3 Complete the sentences with the six words that you did not use in exercise 2.

1 In a buyer's market, _____ exceeds demand.
2 Plans are being discussed for a new engineering _____.
3 Paul got his idea for the new business when he bought _____ toy in a market in Bolivia.
4 Fresh dairy _____ is available from farm shops throughout the country.
5 We must increase our _____ in order to meet all the orders that we have received.
6 _____ to customers in the north are made on Wednesdays and Fridays.

Production philosophies

4 Match the words in column A with their definitions in column B.

A	B
1 raw materials	A a detailed list of items
2 loading bay	B the area where production takes place
3 factory floor	C the cost of keeping goods in a warehouse
4 storage costs	D the time from getting an order to producing the goods
5 waste	E making something better
6 improvement	F the area where goods are delivered or taken away
7 defects	G inefficient or unnecessary use of substances, time, energy and money
8 inventory	H goods, materials or components in the warehouse
9 response time	I imperfections or faults
10 stock	J the basic supplies or resources used to produce goods

5 Work in pairs. Which of the words (1–10) above are places? Which are physical items, and which one is a financial item?

6 What do you know about the 'Just-in-Time' production concept? Work in groups of three and compare your ideas.

7 Read this article taken from a business management journal. Underline the words from column A in exercise 4.

JUST-IN-TIME

The Just-in-Time (JIT) concept was introduced by the Ford Motor Company in the 1950s, and it was based on a very simple idea: raw materials coming into a factory were not taken to a warehouse, but went directly from the loading bay to the factory floor. This eliminated the storage costs of keeping a supply of materials in the warehouse.

Next, the JIT concept was adopted and developed by Dr Shigeo Shingo and Mr Taiichi Ohno of the Toyota Motor Corporation, and it became known as the Toyota Production System. Its key features were the elimination of all waste and the continuous improvement of productivity.

Today the companies that apply a JIT philosophy have learnt a lot from the American and the Japanese experiences. The concept of JIT can be applied to any business, from making cars to preparing food. Its main objective is to improve quality to achieve the highest standards, in other words to have 'zero defects' and to keep costs to a minimum. The principle of JIT may be expressed as: having the right amount of the right material, in the right place, at the right time.

The latest version of JIT is called 'lean manufacturing', in which seven types of waste have been eliminated. These are: overproduction, excess transportation, excess inventory, waiting time, processing, motion and production defects.

When all this waste has been eliminated, the effects can be seen immediately: production is started because there is a demand, products are made and sold, the response time to production is reduced, the financial return is immediate, new stock is ordered when stock reaches the reorder level, the risk of error decreases, and the quality and customer satisfaction improve.

Exam Success

Prepare for Part Five of the Reading Test by reading longer texts (300–400 words) and identifying:
• the main idea of each paragraph.
• the purpose of the text (to give an opinion, etc).
• factual information.

8 Read the article again and answer the following questions.

1 What was done at Ford Motor company to eliminate storage costs?
2 What name was given to the JIT concept at the Toyota Motor Corporation?
3 What is the main objective of JIT?
4 How many sorts of waste have been eliminated in lean manufacturing? What are they?
5 Which sentence in the text summarises the JIT philosophy?

9 Work in groups of four. Decide how the JIT concept could be applied in your company. Then form new groups and compare your ideas.

8.2 Problems and solutions

Solving problems

Language Tip

Poka-Yoke is a Japanese term. It was developed as part of the Toyota Production System, as a mechanism to prevent or detect defects.

1 Look at the photograph and choose the correct caption (A–C) to describe the Poka-Yoke mechanism it shows.

A The use of colourful envelopes means that customers know who letters are from.

B The address window on envelopes stops letters going to the wrong person. It saves time and money as no labels are needed.

C Printing addresses on envelopes saves time, as administrative staff don't need to write addresses by hand.

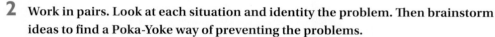

2 Work in pairs. Look at each situation and identity the problem. Then brainstorm ideas to find a Poka-Yoke way of preventing the problems.

3 🔊 8.1 Listen to the lecture at a business school and check your answers to exercise 2.

4 🔊 8.1 Complete the sentences.

1 Poka-yoke mechanisms *can prevent* _____.
2 The tube is designed *so that* _____.
3 Optical cells *stop* _____.
4 The stone is used *to* _____.

5 🔊 8.1 Listen to the lecture again and check your answers.

6 Work in pairs. Say how the items below solve problems or give solutions at work. Try to use the expressions *prevent, stop, so that* or *to*. Be careful with the verb forms.

voicemail	pagers
closed circuit television (CCTV)	smoke detectors/alarms
conference phones	barcode scanners

7 Look at the photograph. What is the special feature of the disposable cup and lid?

8 Read the article and check your answer.

Use a
SMART LID

Have you ever burned your lips by drinking very hot coffee? Then you will understand the value of a 'Smart Lid' cup of coffee.

This lid fits onto a typical disposable cup that you get at airports and other drinks outlets. The lid is manufactured with a temperature-sensitive additive. Before the lid is put onto the cup, it is coffee-coloured. When the lid heats up, the additive changes colour and the lid turns red: the user is warned to be careful of the hot liquid. When the drink cools, the colour of the lid changes back to brown.

The Smart Lid has another excellent feature. When it is put on correctly, there is a complete brown ring around the lid. If the lid is not put on correctly, this ring is incomplete. This gives the user an additional warning that the hot liquid could spill out of the cup.

when and *if*

We use *when* for things that are sure to happen and *if* for things that may happen. We can use both words to show the cause–effect relationship between two facts.

9 Underline the sentences in the article above that begin with *When* and *If.* Answer these questions.

1 Which tense is used in these sentences?
2 Which part of the sentence includes *When/If* – the cause or the effect?

10 Complete the sentences using the verbs in brackets.

1 If the lid is hot, it _____ (turn).
2 When coffee is too hot, you _____ (burn).
3 If ice heats up, it _____ (melt).
4 If you heat water to 100ºC, it _____ (boil).
5 When you switch on the air conditioning, _____ (cool).
6 If you don't plug in the printer, _____ (not work).
7 When we work overtime, _____ (pay).
8 If you have an anti-virus program, _____ (protect).

Collocations with *problem*

1 There are a number of verbs that collocate with the noun *problem*. Complete the sentences with the correct verbs from the box. You can use more than one verb in some of the sentences.

avoid cause deal with detect explain have solve

1 As a production manager, I try to _____ problems as soon as possible. I have to meet my production targets!
2 The new machinery we installed is _____ some problems. I don't think it is compatible with the old system.
3 Jan, can you help me? I'm _____ a problem logging onto the computer system.
4 Well, I'm sure I'll be able to help you if you _____ the problem clearly.
5 I think it's a good idea to try out the new system at the weekend. That way we can _____ any problems with our customers.
6 I enjoy working in customer services – it's true that we _____ problems all day, but it's very satisfying when we can _____ someone's problem.

We've got a problem

2 At Txoklat, a biscuit company, David, the production manager and Angela, the plant manager, are discussing a problem. Read what David says. Then complete the conversation with the sentences in the box.

OK, I'll contact Head Office immediately.	Is it serious?
Oh no! Have you stopped production?	Oh, what's wrong, exactly?
Yes, I'll do that too.	Hi, David. Is something wrong?

Angela (1) _____
David Yes, I think we've got a problem with our Txoko-cake line.
Angela (2) _____
David Yes, I'm afraid it is.
Angela (3) _____
David Some kind of bacteria has been found in one of the machines.
Angela (4) _____
David Yes, of course. We're trying to find the cause of the problem right now.
Angela (5) _____
David Could you tell the laboratory as well, please? They could help us.
Angela (6) _____

3 🔊 8.2 Listen to the conversation and check your answers.

4 Work in pairs.

Student A: Go to page 127.

Student B: First, choose one of the problems below and explain the problem to Student A. Then listen to Student A's problem and make suggestions. Use the expressions from exercise 2.

1 Your computers keep crashing. No information is lost, but this wastes time and your staff are feeling very frustrated.

2 Half of your staff are off sick with flu. It's the end of the month and the accounts need to be done.

3 The electricity supply keeps going off. It is only off for a few minutes each time, but everyone's work is interrupted – and this costs money.

Student A: Go to page 127.

Learning Tip

Improve your speaking confidence by:
• practising conversations with different partners.
• learning useful expressions, eg for agreeing and disagreeing, and giving and asking for opinions.

Language Tip

A *kiln* is an industrial oven.

5 Work in groups of three. Look at the case study. Then read your role cards and follow the instructions.

Student A: You are the production manager.

Student B: You are the maintenance manager.

Student C: You are the purchasing manager.

CASE STUDY

Ceramic plc

Your company makes ceramics. In the last month, production has been stopped five times. The problem is in the kiln where the products are heated. The high temperature needed is not being reached and consequently the ceramics are of poor quality. The production manager has called a meeting to discuss the problem and to find a solution.

ROLE CARD A

Production manager

The constant interruptions in production are costing the company a lot of money. The finished products do not meet industry quality standards, and production targets were not met for last month. The only recent change in the production process was the change in the type of fuel used. You want to go back to the old fuel supplier.

ROLE CARD B

Maintenance manager

You think the problem is either with the quality of the raw materials for the ceramics or with the fuel. You want action to be taken soon because your maintenance workers are spending too long cleaning the kiln. There is other programmed work to be done as well.

ROLE CARD C

Purchasing manager

You are responsible for buying the fuel (coal) for the production process. You got an excellent price on coal from the Far East. You signed a contract for two years. The quality of the coal was guaranteed. You think the kiln is not being maintained properly.

6 Write a memo to the plant manager to report on the conclusions of the meeting. Write 60–80 words.

8.3

Speaking Test: Part Two

In Part Two of the Speaking Test, you have to talk for one minute on a business topic. Each candidate is given two questions, and has to choose one of them to answer. You will have one minute to prepare your talk.

The questions always start: **What is important when...?** After the question, there are three prompts to help you answer.

1 **Here is a typical task from Part Two of the Speaking Test. Which reason (A–C) goes with each of the three prompts?**

> **WHAT IS IMPORTANT WHEN...?**
>
> Choosing a shipping company
> - Speed of service
> - Cost
> - Recommendation from a friend

A A friend can tell you if the company is reliable.

B Fast delivery could be important, depending on the goods to be shipped.

C The price of transport is always an important consideration.

2 **Work in pairs. Think of other reasons for each prompt.**

3 **Which prompt do you think is most important when choosing a shipping company?**

4 **Work in pairs with a different partner. Choose one prompt sheet each.**

Look at the question. Take one minute to prepare your answer. Think of reasons to explain your choice of prompt. Then tell you partner your answer.

> **WHAT IS IMPORTANT WHEN...?**
>
> Booking an international flight for a business trip
> - Departure times
> - In-flight service
> - Price of the ticket

> **WHAT IS IMPORTANT WHEN...?**
>
> Choosing a meal with an important client
> - Price
> - Type of food
> - Quality of service

Speaking Test: Part Three

In Part Three of the Speaking Test, the examiner describes a scenario and gives you some information (a text or some pictures) to look at. You must discuss the situation with the other candidate and try to come to a joint decision. The examiner will then ask you further questions relating to the main theme.

5 Here is a typical example of the information the examiner will read out to you.

> **Scenario:**
>
> Your bank is organising an English course for its staff. Talk together about which staff should do the course, and why, as well as which staff don't need it. Decide which three groups of staff should do the course.

The examiner will then give you a prompt sheet (either prompts like those below, or pictures). Work in pairs. Look at these prompts. Talk together for two minutes and decide which three groups of staff would benefit most from the course.

> **Bank staff include:**
>
> • Cashiers
> • Credit card administrators
> • Branch managers
> • Security guards
> • Receptionists/Telephonists
>
> • Human resources staff
> • IT systems staff
> • Quality department staff
> • Cleaning and maintenance staff
> • Foreign exchange department staff

6 Work in pairs. Discuss these questions.

1 Apart from business English, what other courses do companies arrange for their staff?

2 Have you ever been on any courses arranged by your company/school? What did you get from the course?

3 Is there a course that you would particularly like to do? What is the topic? Why would you like to do this course?

9.1

The future

READING

1 **Match the words (1–8) with their definitions (A–H).**

1 prototype
2 fuel
3 green
4 the norm
5 exhaust emission
6 on the market
7 hybrid
8 run on

A a mixture of things
B for sale
C use as an energy source
D the first model of something
E the gases produced when an engine uses fuel
F typical or usual
G something which produces energy when burned
H does not harm the environment

2 **Read the press release quickly and choose the best title.**

A French cars pollute the least
B Hydrogen engine ready for production
C Petrol reserves to run out

PRESS RELEASE

HydroHybrid announced this week that a fully-working version of their new hydrogen engine is now ready to go into production.

With several years' experience in manufacturing power generators that run on hydrogen, the company started developing a prototype car engine three years ago.

HydroHybrid's Marketing Director, Jason Marsh, said, 'We decided to develop the hydrogen engine because that's the future as far as cars are concerned; petrol is the fuel of the past. Consumers are more aware of the environment these days and they are going to demand 'green' alternatives. We're convinced that hydrogen engines are going to be the key to our car-oriented lifestyle. Filling your tank with hydrogen will soon be the norm.'

The engine will make a significant contribution to reducing pollution, since, by using hydrogen as fuel, the only exhaust emission will be water.

HydroHybrid recently started negotiations with a French car manufacturer to put the new engine into one of their models. 'We will have a trial version by the end of next year,' the MD added, 'and if everything runs smoothly, the car will be on the market in 12 to 18 months.'

And the good news is that car owners won't have to wait until hydrogen suppliers are on every corner: the engine is a hybrid, so, as well as hydrogen, it will also run on petrol.

Learning Tip

Increase your reading skills by reading longer texts for pleasure. Read about things that interest you, and don't use a dictionary except when really necessary.

3 **Read the press release again. Decide whether these sentences are 'Right' or 'Wrong'. If there isn't enough information to answer 'Right' or 'Wrong', choose 'Doesn't say'.**

1 HydroHybrid's prototype engine will be ready in three years.
   A Right   B Wrong   C Doesn't say
2 The HydroHybrid engine will produce no exhaust emissions.
   A Right   B Wrong   C Doesn't say
3 Demand for the hydrogen engine in France is already high.
   A Right   B Wrong   C Doesn't say
4 A car containing the HydroHybrid engine will be available in less than a year.
   A Right   B Wrong   C Doesn't say

The future: *will* for predictions

In Unit 2, you practised the present continuous (for fixed arrangements in the future) and in Unit 5 *going to* (for intentions). In Unit 4, you used *will* to make offers and promises.

We often use *will* to make predictions about the future.
*Filling your tank with hydrogen **will** soon **be** the norm.*

Note that we can also use *going to* to make predictions – but only when we can see, or we have evidence, that the action is sure to happen.
*Consumers are more aware of the environment these days and they **are going to demand** 'green' alternatives.*

4 **Read these predictions. Say if you agree or disagree, and why.**

  0 Trams will replace buses in city centres.
     I don't think trams will replace buses in our city. That's unrealistic.
  1 Cars with only one occupant won't be allowed into city centres.
  2 Public transport will be free for children up to the age of 16.
  3 Low-cost airlines won't be able to offer cheap flights because of high taxes on fuel.
  4 High-speed trains will link all major cities.

5 **Use these notes to make predictions. Work in small groups.**

  0 horses replacing cars
     I think we'll start using horses again instead of cars – there won't be any petrol for domestic use!
  1 bigger planes
  2 alternative 'green' fuels
  3 domestic solar panels
  4 changes to local weather
  5 different holiday destinations

The first conditional

We can also make predictions about the future based on conditions.
*If everything runs smoothly, the car **will be** on the market in 12 to 18 months.*

First conditional sentences tell us what may happen in the future. The result (the main clause) depends on the condition stated in the *if*-clause. The verb in the *if*-clause is in the present tense and the verb in the main clause is *will* + infinitive.

Note that first conditional sentences can begin with either clause.
*The world will be a 'greener' place **if** the hydrogen car becomes popular.*

6 **Use your ideas from exercise 5 to write sentences with the first conditional.**

If horses replace cars, I will get a job near my house.

7 **Complete these sentences with your own ideas. Compare with a partner.**

  1 If I _____ (finish) work early tonight, _____
  2 We _____ (get) paid a bonus next month if _____
  3 My boss _____ (be) angry tomorrow morning if _____
  4 If our department _____ (meet) its targets this month,

     _____

  5 If you _____ (arrive) late for work again, _____
  6 I _____ (look for) another job if _____

Strategies for the future

1 **Match the beginnings of the sentences (1–6) with the endings (A–F) to make complete sentences.**

1 To enter the Chinese market we need to form a *joint*
2 The favourable euro–dollar *exchange*
3 Travellers on *low*
4 The new high-speed train uses *state-of-the-art*
5 The price of fuel was a *key*
6 CO2 levels will continue to rise in *the near*

A *rate* means that our imports are cheaper.
B *future*, and then they will start to fall.
C *cost* airlines spend more money in airports.
D *factor* when deciding which vehicles to buy.
E *venture* with a local company.
F *technology* to predict journey times.

2 **Use three of the expressions in *italics* in sentences of your own.**

3 **Auro Construction (AC) builds electricity generation plants. Look at the Executive summary of the Strategy Briefing Document and decide which change the company is considering.**

A Closing European operations
B Expanding into the Chinese market
C Withdrawing from the Chinese market

Strategy Briefing Document

Executive summary

Over the last few years, the demand for electricity in China has increased dramatically. At the same time, demand here in Europe has stabilised and it is unlikely that it will increase greatly in the future. We currently operate only in Europe and we need to consider our future operations.

- Does Europe give us any potential for growth?
- Is this the right time to go ahead with expansion?
- What are the market conditions in other geographical areas?

It is essential to make a correct assessment of future opportunities. In Section A of this Briefing document, a PEST analysis looks at the external factors which will affect our future strategy decisions.

Section A PEST ANALYSIS

(1) _____

The Chinese government allows foreign companies to invest in China only if they form joint ventures with Chinese companies; this is unlikely to change in the near future. On the other hand, China is promoting foreign trade which is of 'mutual benefit'.

(2) _____

Investments in China are attractive because of the low costs, especially of raw materials. However, foreign exchange transactions are controlled by the relevant Chinese laws. The tax situation is complex.

(3) _____

Lifestyles are changing very quickly in China; this is causing a dramatic rise in the demand for low-cost electricity, but today only a small percentage of Chinese have sufficient electricity for their needs. The electricity market in this country is likely to grow for at least the next 20 years.

(4) _____

There are special low tax rates for joint ventures that use advanced technology. The technology and equipment must be appropriate for China's needs.

From the above factors, we suggest that starting up new operations in China is a viable option for AC. We need to do further research into this, with a view to setting up a joint venture with a Chinese company.

4 **Read the rest of the document and match the headings with the paragraphs (1–4). What is a PEST analysis?**

Economic   Technological   Political   Social

5 Choose the best ending (A, B or C) for each sentence (1–4).

1 AC has done a PEST analysis to
   A predict future business opportunities.
   B analyse the present financial situation.
   C assess current operations.
2 Foreign companies can invest in China only if
   A they are unlikely to change in the near future.
   B they establish a joint venture with a Chinese company.
   C their trade is of mutual benefit to China and the foreign company.
3 The growth of the energy market in China is the result of
   A the rapid changes in lifestyle.
   B the small market in China at the moment.
   C the low cost of electricity.
4 In China, using advanced technology
   A is essential in a joint venture.
   B brings financial advantages.
   C is not appropriate.

LISTENING

A strategy meeting

6 9.1 Now listen to part of the AC strategy meeting and complete the notes for the Legal and Environmental analysis. Compare with a partner.

Legal	*Environmental*
Things are _____	China will need _____
The situation is _____	The areas where AC could build plants are not _____

7 Look at the comments from participants in the AC strategy meeting. Match the sentence beginnings (1–6) with the endings (A–F) to make complete sentences. Decide if the sentences are for or against the expansion plan.

1 The demand in China will grow
2 If we don't set up a joint venture, we won't
3 I don't think the exchange rates will stay
4 We'll have to cut our costs dramatically if we want to
5 Are we sure that demand in Europe won't
6 If we don't take this opportunity,

A as favourable.
B increase with EU expansion?
C even faster than we expect.
D compete with local providers.
E other companies will get there before us.
F be able to operate there successfully.

8 Work individually. Using the information from the PESTLE (PEST + Legal and Environmental) analysis and the ideas in exercise 7, prepare a short presentation in favour of or against the AC expansion plan. Give the presentation to two other students.

9.2 Meetings

1 Read this item from an online news service. What damage has the storm caused?

Tropical storm hits Poland

Hurricane Kyrill killed six people and left dozens injured as it swept across Poland. Up to a million people were without electricity this morning, and the damage to public buildings and homes is still being assessed.

The dead include a crane operator whose crane was blown over by the hurricane force winds. Falling trees caused much of the structural damage, and brought down power and communications lines.

The authorities have advised people to stay indoors and to avoid travelling if possible since both road and rail links are severely disrupted, especially in the southern and western regions. Emergency teams are working to restore telephone lines and power to key sectors, and the army is clearing the roads.

The main force of the hurricane has now passed, although strong winds will continue until tomorrow.

Crisis meeting

2 9.2 Auro Construction owns a subsidiary, AC Polonia, in Poland. Listen to the crisis meeting between Ludovica (the plant manager), Davide (the general manager) and Mirko (the IT manager). Choose the correct answer (A, B or C) for each question.

1 How many crisis meetings have the management had today?
 A three
 B four
 C more than four

2 Marek was calling from
 A a mobile.
 B somebody else's phone.
 C the Polish plant, but the line was bad.

3 Marek said that
 A the workers on the night shift were evacuated and somebody was hurt.
 B nobody was hurt, but the workers were evacuated during the night.
 C a number of night shift workers were hurt.

4 The first thing they decide to do is
 A assess the damage to the factory.
 B limit the loss of production.
 C stop production in the factory.

5 Who do they decide to send to assess the damage?
 A Ludovica
 B Marek or Pavel
 C Jonathan

6 Mirko says the Polish plant can
 A connect to the Internet if they have mobile phones.
 B send an email with the production data.
 C repair the telephone lines easily.

3 Complete this email with the missing action points.

To: Davide Ferrari
From: Ludovica Bianchi
Davide,
Just to give you an update on the action points from the Poland meeting. I've checked with the planning department and they say we can move production to the German plant. I've called (**1**) _____ to tell him this. We are sending (**2**) _____ to Poland – he will be there early this afternoon. When we get a report from him, we'll know exactly what happened, and I'll send (**3**) _____ to start the repair work.
Let me know if there is anything else,
Ludovica

4 9.2 Listen to the meeting again and check your answers.

GRAMMAR

will + time clauses

5 Complete these sentences with *when* or *if*. Which sentence expresses a certainty? Which sentence expresses a possibility? Which tense follows *when*?

1 _____ we know what happened exactly, I'll send a small team.
2 _____ they have a couple of mobile phones, they can connect up to the Internet.

6 Which option is not correct in each sentence?

1 *As soon as / When / Before* we get the damage assessment, we'll draw up a plan.
2 *When / Until / After* the wind drops, we'll try to fix the roof.
3 We'll be back online *when / as soon as / until* the phone line is restored.
4 I'll start the repair work *before / if / as soon as* everything is ready.

SPEAKING

Brainstorming

7 People face different problems at work, ranging from the trivial to life-threatening. Which of the following problems need a crisis meeting to discuss them? Compare with your partner.

a faulty coffee machine	a steady loss of clients
new anti-smoking laws	suppliers on strike
too few administrative staff	a subcontractor goes bankrupt

8 Work in groups of four. Think of a problem affecting your company or your workplace. Hold a brainstorming meeting to find solutions. Note down the action points you decide on.

Useful language	
The first thing we have to do is …	You'll have to …
When we know …	I'll …
Let's …	

9 Write an email to your manager confirming the action points decided at the meeting and stating who will do them. Write 30–40 words.

Crisis strategy

1 Complete the sentences about business crises using the words in the box.

> fight   collapsed   damaged   cost   hit

1 Share prices _____ last night following the US political crisis.
2 The retail sector was _____ hard when interest rates went up again this month.
3 Enron's reputation was _____ after the allegations of financial malpractice.
4 The salmonella incident _____ the poultry industry millions in lost sales.
5 UK banks will _____ back after online fraud chaos.

2 Companies need a strategy to deal with a crisis. Put the four steps (a–d) of a typical crisis communication plan in order.

a Decide who will be responsible for handling the crisis.
b Decide who will be the point of contact between your Crisis Team and the media.
c Collect information and make sure you know the relevant facts.
d Identify who you need to communicate with: your customers, the media, etc.

3 9.3 Listen to a podcast by Ellis Whims, a PR expert, and check your answers to exercise 2.

4 9.3 Listen again and complete the missing information.

1 Every organisation needs a _____.
2 A crisis plan enables a company to handle a crisis quickly and _____.
3 First, collect information about the _____.
4 Second, appoint a _____ to handle the crisis.
5 Third, appoint a _____ to be the contact between the crisis team and the media.
6 Fourth, identify your key _____: your customers, employees, salespeople and the media.

5 Do you know what to do in a crisis? Can you remember the advice that Ellis Whims gave?

Student A: Close your book and tell Student B what steps to follow.

Student B: Listen to your partner and check the information.

Exam Success

This exercise is similar to Part Three of the Listening Test. Before you listen, remember to read all the information, and try and predict what is missing.

Collocations with *meeting*

6 Put each word into the correct group (1–3).

> ~~attend~~ arrange ~~agenda~~ action points ~~board~~ chair crisis
> chairperson departmental hold minutes miss run team

1 types of meeting   *board*
2 verbs connected to meetings   *attend*
3 nouns connected to meetings   *agenda*

7 Write a word in each gap.

1 Can you take the _____, please?
2 How many people usually _____ the meetings?
3 Can we move on to the next item on the _____?
4 Where's Olga? She will _____ the meeting if she doesn't get here soon.
5 Can we _____ a different time for the next meeting?

8 One of your important customers and his client suffered food poisoning at your restaurant recently. You have seen this letter of complaint in a specialist catering magazine. Your business partner has just informed you that this bad review and an Internet blog are affecting business and bookings are down 50 per cent. Hold a meeting with your business partner and decide what to do. Use the strategy from exercises 2–4 to make a crisis communications plan. Use the Useful language on page 91 to help you.

> and after waiting at our table for about thirty minutes, our waiter finally returned to take our order. We both ordered fish soup, which was tasteless and far too hot, as we discovered when the waiter spilled most of it over both the table and ourselves. The main courses, of steak tartare and lamb chops, were not very good either. The only good thing about the meal was the top quality fresh cream desserts and perfect coffee. After the terrible service and poor food, we were happy to leave and forget all about the experience. But later that evening, I'm afraid things went from bad to worse

Letter of apology

9 One of your action points from the meeting is to write to the customer. Read the letter of complaint again and write a letter of apology from the restaurant management, including the information below. Write about 60–80 words.

- apologise for the poor service
- apologise for the food poisoning incident
- accept full responsibility
- offer a complimentary dinner for two

9.3

Reading Test: Part Four

In Part Four of the Reading Test, you have to read a text and decide whether each statement is right or wrong, or if the information isn't given. You will need to work out the meaning of unknown words from context in order to do this.

- First, read the heading and try to predict what the article is about.
- Then, scan the text quickly. Think about where it comes from and who it is for.
- Next, read the questions, and underline important words.
- Now read the text carefully. Underline important words.
- Read the questions again, and answer the ones you're sure about.
- Then read the text again, and try to find the words that help you to answer the other questions.

Here is an exam task from Part Four. Read the instructions and do the task.

PART FOUR

- Read the newspaper article below about a bank in Bangladesh.
- Are sentences 1–5 'Right' or 'Wrong'? If there is not enough information to answer 'Right' or 'Wrong', choose 'Doesn't say'.

Giving loans to the poor

The Grameen Bank is an organisation started in Bangladesh that makes small loans (known as micro-credit) to poor people, without asking for collateral. The system is based on the idea that the poor have skills that are under-used. The bank also accepts deposits, provides other services, and runs several development-oriented businesses including telephone and energy companies.

In 1974, Muhammad Yunus, who founded the bank, gave a small loan of $27 to a group of families so that they could make small items for sale, without extremely high interest rates. Yunus believed that giving this micro-credit to a wide population could reduce poverty in the rural areas of Bangladesh.

1   The bank's customers must have property to guarantee a loan.
    A Right   B Wrong   C Doesn't say
2   Giving loans is not the bank's only line of business.
    A Right   B Wrong   C Doesn't say
3   The maximum loan given to anyone is $27.
    A Right   B Wrong   C Doesn't say
4   The bank always charges extremely high interest rates.
    A Right   B Wrong   C Doesn't say
5   All of the bank's clients live in rural areas of Bangladesh.
    A Right   B Wrong   C Doesn't say

Reading Test: Part Five

EXAM FORMAT

In Part Five of the Reading Test, you have to choose the correct answers from three options. You will need to extract relevant information, read for both general sense and detail, scan for specific information, and understand the writer's purpose.

APPROACH

- First, read the heading and try to predict what the article is about.
- Then, scan the text quickly. Think about where it comes from and who it is for.
- Next, read the questions, and underline important words.
- Now read the text carefully. Underline important words.
- Then read the text again, and try to find the words that help you to identify the correct answer or to identify the incorrect answers.
- Remember: the questions come in the same order as the information in the text.

EXAM PRACTICE

Exam Success

Parts Five and Six of the Reading Test both have multiple choice questions.
- Choose the option you think is correct.
- Check that the other two options are incorrect.

2 Here is a typical task from Part Five. Read the instructions and do the task.

PART FIVE
- Read the following newspaper article about telecommuting.
- For each question **1–4**, choose the correct answer (**A**, **B** or **C**).

Telecommuting

Working at home and saving money at the same time might sound too good to be true, but more and more people are now telecommuting – working from home using the Internet.

One of the reasons why this has become popular is that people are tired of commuting. But the benefits are not only for the employees, as both parties have a lot to gain.

Employers benefit because employees are less likely to take time off. Employees who work from home generally suffer from less stress because they have more time. The time that they gain from not commuting means that they often feel there is a better balance between their work and their life.

However, although telecommuting is popular with both companies and employees, it means that middle management have to change their management style, since they don't have so much direct contact with the employees. There is a danger that managers focus too much on results; they have to find new ways of motivating and maintaining close contact with their staff.

Another advantage for employees is that they can work more flexible hours. This means they can take their children to school and be at home when the children finish school, instead of the children spending long hours in after-school care.

Telecommuters have to be self-motivated and have a good productivity record, and they should also have enough discipline to know when to start and stop working. Employees who work at home can be more productive than their office colleagues because they have fewer distractions.

1 According to the article, telecommuting is popular because people

   A like using the Internet.

   B like working from home.

   C don't like travelling to work every day.

2 According to the article, employers benefit from telecommuting because

   A employees take fewer days off.

   B they save on the cost of offices.

   C they can take time off.

3 Middle managers

   A don't like telecommuting.

   B don't usually work from home.

   C need to change the way they manage telecommuters.

4 According to the article, telecommuters need

   A to be good parents.

   B self-discipline.

   C to work harder than their office colleagues.

10.1   Career development

Business skills portfolio

1   Read the Chamber of Commerce website. Who are the courses for?

   A   people looking for their first job

   B   students in full-time education

   C   people already in jobs

Chamber of Commerce Business Skills Portfolio

Education in the workplace

Professional development courses: autumn/winter programme

[seminars (full or half day)]   [semester courses]   [e-learning]

Click on the title for more information and dates offered or call 091 774 878

Time management and how to prioritise

Don't just manage, lead!

Successful customer management

Effective communication skills for results

Creativity and innovation – mind gymnastics

2   Read more from the Business Skills Portfolio website and decide which words could fill the gaps (1–8). Then choose the correct options from the list below.

The Chamber of Commerce Business Skills Portfolio gives you high quality, value for money training opportunities. **(1)** _____ days, employers understand that employees who are given training and development opportunities are more motivated **(2)** _____ contribute more to the company. **(3)** _____ courses cover a wide range of subjects and cost from as little as £170. They are designed specifically to develop employees' skills, and at the same time they **(4)** _____ businesses increase efficiency and profitability. All of our courses are led by professional trainers **(5)** _____ extensive expertise and understanding of business needs.

We offer:

seminars which run for a full or half day, and give you the skills you need **(6)** _____ and effectively;

semester courses where you attend lectures or seminars once a week over a three-month period;

e-learning which gives all the flexibility a busy **(7)** _____ needs.

The qualifications you get will depend on the type of training. You **(8)** _____ find more information under each course title.

1	A Those	B This	C These
2	A and	B but	C with
3	A Your	B Our	C His
4	A helps	B helped	C help
5	A with	B of	C from
6	A quickly	B quicker	C quick
7	A persons	B people	C person
8	A can	B going to	C are

Relative clauses

3 Relative clauses give extra information about people and things. Look again at the text in exercise 2 and find the answers to questions 1 and 2. Complete the sentences.

    1 What kind of employees are more motivated?

      Employees _____ are more motivated.

    2 What kind of seminars do they offer?

      We offer seminars _____.

4 Underline the relative pronouns in the sentences you completed in exercise 3.

5 Relative pronouns introduce relative clauses. In the sentences below, underline the relative clause and circle the person or thing it gives information about.

    0 I'm doing a course which is internationally recognised.

    1 I've always had bosses who knew how to motivate people.

    2 I enjoy working for a company which values its employees.

    3 We could choose the sessions which were most useful to us.

    4 My manager is someone who always gets good results.

> Note: *who* and *that* can both be used for people, but we usually say *who*; *which* and *that* can both be used for things.
>
> We also use the relative pronouns *where* and *whose* for places and possessives.
> *It's lovely to work in an office **where** we have natural light all day.*
> *The woman **whose** department met all its targets is being promoted.*

6 Write a relative pronoun (*who, which, where, whose*) in the gaps.

    1 I need a course _____ gives me lots of flexibility because I travel a lot.

    2 I enjoy learning things _____ help me in my job.

    3 The lecture theatre _____ we usually go is too small for so many people.

    4 Employees _____ do career development courses earn more money.

    5 There isn't a TV screen in the room _____ we do this course.

    6 I know lots of students _____ grades are better than mine!

    7 The speaker _____ gave the talk is very well known.

    8 The lecturer _____ course I'm doing was on TV last night.

    9 The session _____ follows this one looks very interesting.

    10 People _____ arrive late are not admitted to the sessions.

> Sometimes we can leave out *who, which* or *that* if it is not the subject of the verb.
> *The seminar **(that)** I went to was well attended.* (*The seminar* is not the subject of the verb *went*.)
> *The trainer **who** led the session was really dynamic.* (*The trainer* is the subject of the verb *led*.)

7 Put brackets around the relative pronouns that can be left out.

    0 The timetable (which) I chose gave me lots of free time.

    1 The trainer who we had also works in our company.

    2 The prices that they charge are quite reasonable.

    3 That's the course which I attended last year.

    4 The man who took my application form was in my group.

    5 The qualifications which you get will depend on the type of training.

Creativity and leadership

1 **10.1** **Listen to the introduction to a workshop on *Creativity and innovation – mind gymnastics* and choose the best ending for each sentence.**

1 The workshop today will have

   A two sessions.   B three sessions.   C four sessions.

2 The workshop will look at activities

   A to do with colleagues at work.

   B which increase your creativity.

   C that increase your profits.

3 The trainer says that scientists believe that changes to your daily routine can

   A make you cleverer, more confident and better at making decisions.

   B help you live longer and more healthily.

   C make your life and work more interesting than it was before.

4 In the first session of the workshop, the trainer will explain

   A ten simple activities.

   B seven mental exercises.

   C one activity to do this week.

2 **Work in pairs. Look at the handout below and think of ways to complete the information. Use these ideas.**

a friend	meditation class	a crossword puzzle
alcohol	ten phone numbers	the wrong hand
clothes	tuna or salmon	words from a dictionary
plant	your eyes closed	your shopping list
stranger	your workplace	pictures for your walls

Creativity and Innovation – **Mind Gymnastics**

Daily activities for increased brain power

1 have a shower with _____

2 brush your teeth with _____

3 change your normal route to _____

4 choose some new _____

5 go to a yoga or _____

6 memorise _____

7 do a Sudoku or _____

8 talk to _____

9 eat fish, such as _____

10 have no caffeine and no _____

3 **10.2** **Listen to the trainer and check your answers.**

4 **Do you think this kind of activity can affect your brain power? Choose seven of the activities – and do one each day, next week. Compare with your partner. Discuss how you could measure the success of the activities. Use these ideas and your own.**

Do an IQ test before and after activities.   Compare how confident you feel.

Test your memory.   Assess your decision-making skills.

Compare how you perform at work.

Describing people

5 Think of a good leader you have known, or a leader in public life. Which of the statements below describe the person? Tell your partner about the person, using these sentences or ideas of your own.

He/She was a very charismatic / dynamic / ambitious / organised / open person.
He/She was good at motivating people / communicating / listening.
He/She was confident / understanding / patient / creative / authoritative.

6 Match the sentence patterns with the examples above and write an example for each one from your comments in exercise 5.

1 *be good at* + verb + *-ing*
2 *be a* + adjective + noun
3 *be* + adjective

7 Would you make a good leader? Complete the questionnaire. Then go to page 129 to interpret the results.

Don't just manage, lead! Do you have leadership potential?	strongly disagree	disagree	neither agree nor disagree	agree	strongly agree
1 People count on me for ideas.	1	2	3	4	5
2 It's important to me to build a united team.	1	2	3	4	5
3 The success of my team is more important to me than my own personal success.	1	2	3	4	5
4 I give praise and positive feedback to others.	1	2	3	4	5
5 I listen to other people's ideas.	1	2	3	4	5
6 I like people to do what I say.	1	2	3	4	5
7 I like to resolve disagreements between people.	1	2	3	4	5
8 I encourage people to be creative individuals.	1	2	3	4	5
9 I like taking responsibility for decisions.	1	2	3	4	5
10 People describe me with words like 'focused, motivating, inspiring', etc.	1	2	3	4	5
TOTAL					

Learning Tip

Write down your ideas when you are preparing for both speaking and writing. Write as many ideas as you can. Then select the most useful ones for your speaking or writing.

8 Write down the three most important characteristics of leaders. Compare with your partner and agree on three, discarding some ideas if necessary. Compare with another pair, and again agree on the three most important points. Write three sentences to summarise your conclusions. Read your classmates' sentences. Do you all agree?

A good leader is someone who …

10.2 Organising a conference

Collocations

1 Match words from group A with words from group B to fit the definitions (1–6).

A	B
development	venture
enrolment	speaker
keynote	fee
multi-sectorial	form
new	agency
speaker's	event

1 a person who gives the main talk at an event
2 an organisation which promotes expansion and growth
3 a project or business which is just beginning
4 a document where you give your details to participate in an event
5 an occasion when companies from different areas of business meet
6 the payment which an invited presenter or lecturer receives

What's still to do?

2 🔘 **10.3** CityActive is a development agency which promotes and assists business initiatives in Dublin. Together with the Chamber of Commerce they are organising a multi-sectorial conference to help local businesses to network. Look at the conference organiser's 'to do' list. Listen to the meeting between the organiser, Tracey, and her boss, Burton. Tick the things Tracey has already done.

> DUBLIN ENTERPRISE DAYS: New Ventures and Networking
> To do
> confirm date
> book rooms at City Conference Centre
> send programme to printers
> confirm conference speakers
> set up online registration form
> arrange promotion and advertising
> arrange catering
> finalise budget

3 🔘 **10.3** Listen again and complete the missing information using a word or numbers.

> conference dates: _____
>
> conference times: _____
>
> conference rooms: _____
>
> type of catering: _____

4 Which of the uncompleted tasks is the priority?

5 Work in groups of three. Read about the available speakers and decide which one to invite to the conference.

▲ **Gregor Rose**
Professor of Human Interaction, Stirling University, Scotland
Specialist areas:
  analysis of successful networks
  fostering an entrepreneurial culture
  social issues in e-commerce

▲ **Eva Hanson**
Founder and owner, Perfect Perfumes, Bonn, Germany
Specialist areas:
  modern entrepreneurship
  starting small, being successful
  new business initiatives

▲ **Craig Nicholson**
Director, Inter-Act Agency, Belfast
Specialist areas:
  leading from the front
  new ways for new business
  strategic planning

6 Write an email to invite the speaker you chose in exercise 5. Give brief details of the conference and a preferred topic for the speech. Write 60–80 words.

> **Useful language**
>
> I am writing to invite you …
> We would be delighted if you could …
> I enclose details of …
> Please confirm …

LISTENING

The conference budget

7 🎧 10.4 The second priority from the planning meeting was to finalise the conference budget. Listen to the meeting between Tracey and her assistant Michelle, and complete the missing figures in Tracey's notes.

> ENTERPRISE DAY BUDGET – problem items
>
> | item | total |
> | --- | --- |
> | conference centre fees | _____ |
> | speakers | _____ |
> | conference packs | _____ |
> | multimedia equipment | _____ (per hour) |

8 🎧 10.4 Listen to the meeting again. Find out what the planners are going to do about going over budget.

9 🎧 10.5 Listen to Michelle's phone call to the City Conference Centre. Make notes while you listen. Compare with a partner.

10 Use your notes to write a short message from Michelle to Tracey, telling her about the outcome of the phone call.

Small talk

1 A representative of CityActive goes to collect the keynote speaker, Eva Hanson, from her hotel. Complete the dialogue with the expressions in the box.

And how was your journey?	No, not at all.
Good morning, Ms Hanson.	That's very kind of you.
Have you been to Ireland before?	Well, shall we set off?

Celia   (**1**) _____ I'm Celia Kirkpatrick from CityActive.

Eva   How do you do? Please call me Eva.

Celia   How do you do, Eva? I hope you haven't been waiting long?

Eva   (**2**) _____ Where I come from, we have a habit of arriving a little early. I was just sitting here admiring the view of the river.

Celia   Yes, we're very proud of our river here in Dublin.
(**3**) _____

Eva   No, this is the first time. Everything is very green, isn't it?

Celia   Yes, thanks to the rain we get, I suppose. By the way, would you like to borrow an umbrella?

Eva   (**4**) _____ I haven't brought one with me.

Celia   (**5**) _____ No delays with the weather, I hope?

Eva   It was fine. There were no problems at all, thanks.

Celia   (**6**) _____ I have a taxi waiting outside.

2 🔘 10.6   **Listen and check your answers to exercise 1.**

3 Work in pairs. Write two other phrases for each gap (1–6) in the conversation in exercise 1.

4 Find a new partner.

Student A: You are visiting from a different country.

Student B: You are the local host.

Make small talk while you travel from the airport to the hotel.

5 Work in groups of four. You are going on an in-company course at the head office in Manchester. How much do you know about doing business in the UK? Decide which of these statements are true in a UK business context. Check your answers on page 129.

1 It's usual to call people by their first names: 'Mr Peter' or 'Ms Anne'.
2 Businessmen wear suits and ties, except on Fridays, when they wear casual clothes.
3 We usually give a small gift the first time we meet someone.
4 For us, a ten o'clock meeting starts at ten o'clock.
5 Typical topics for small talk include politics and earnings.
6 We don't touch other people, except for a handshake when saying 'hello' and 'goodbye'.

6 Discuss each statement with reference to your own culture. What advice about punctuality, small talk and dress code would you give a business visitor to your country?

Exam Success

Part Three of the Speaking Test is a conversation with your partner from prompts. Practise brainstorming ideas on different topics, then talking for about two minutes, using your ideas.

Offers and invitations

7 🔘 10.7 You are going to hear four short conversations between participants at the conference. Read the questions and possible replies. Then listen and tick the reply that is given to each invitation.

1 *Would you like to* join us for dinner?
  A Yes, I'd be delighted.
  B It's very kind of you to ask, but I'm leaving this evening.
  C Thanks, that sounds great.

2 *We're thinking of* doing some sight-seeing this evening. *Are you free?*
  A Good idea, what time shall we meet?
  B Yes, I'd like to join you.
  C Thanks, but I've got a lot of paperwork to do back at the hotel.

3 *Can I offer you* a drink?
  A I'm afraid I don't drink, but a fruit juice would be fine.
  B Yes, please. What is the typical drink here?
  C A beer, please.

4 *Have you tried* the beef? It's a local speciality.
  A I'm sorry, I'm a vegetarian.
  B It looks very nice, thanks.
  C It smells delicious, but I think I prefer the fish.

8 Work in pairs. Practise the exchanges above, using the phrases in *italics* and your own ideas.

A: Would you like to have a drink after the last talk?
B: It's very kind of you to ask, but I'm leaving this evening.

Replying to an invitation

9 Read the email that Eva Hanson received when she got back to work after the conference. Underline the invitation.

Dear Eva,

I thoroughly enjoyed your talk at the conference last week, and it was good to talk to you – briefly – afterwards. I'd be interested to hear more about what your company does. As I said, I'm in your area next week – are you free for lunch one day? Perhaps you can recommend a restaurant near your office.

Laura

Laura Allman
Allman Glass
www.AllmanGlass.com

10 Reply to Laura's email, either accepting or declining the invitation, or suggesting an alternative arrangement.

10.3

EXAM FORMAT

APPROACH

Writing Test: Part Two

In Part Two of the Writing Test, you have to write a longer piece of business correspondence, 60–80 words. You have to write a letter, or an email, which will be sent to someone outside the company. The style will be either formal, or neutral.

- Read the situation carefully.
- Read the task and underline the four points you must cover.
- Think about the person you are writing to, and how formal you should be.
- Think about why you are writing.
- Use appropriate beginnings and endings for the letter/email.
- Keep to the word limit.
- Remember to organise the letter/email in paragraphs.

1 Here is a typical task from Part Two of the Writing Test. Underline the type of communication you have to write and the name of the person you will reply to.

PART TWO
- Read this part of a catering company's advertisement in a local newspaper.

> For 15 years, **Wellington Catering Co.** has provided full, top quality catering services, for those special occasions, from romantic dinners for two, to wedding receptions, to corporate events. We specialise in healthy, Mediterranean food.
> *Just email us for a quotation:*
> Suzy_Brent@wellington.co.uk

- Write **an email** to Ms Brent:
  - referring to the advertisement
  - telling her you are organising an event for your company
  - explaining what type of event it is, and how many people there will be
  - asking her for a quotation, and about discounts for large numbers.
- **Write 60–80 words.**

---

2 Match the beginnings of the sentences (1–5) with the endings (A–E) to make complete sentences.

1 Could you please give me
2 Could you send me details
3 The dinner will be on 20 October
4 I have read your recent
5 We are currently organising

A of the discount you give for large numbers?
B a dinner for some of our clients.
C a quotation for this dinner?
D and there will be approximately 400 people attending.
E advertisement in the Evening News.

3 Which of the sentences in exercise 2 can be written in the same paragraph?

4 Write your answer to the question in exercise 1, using the sentences in exercise 2. Follow the sequence in the instructions. Include an appropriate ending to the email. Remember to structure your email in paragraphs.

Part 2: Write your answer in the box below.

---

5 Here is another typical task from Part Two of the Writing Test. Read the instructions and do the task. Follow the sequence in the instructions.

PART TWO
• Read this part of a letter of complaint from a Mr Prandrakash.

> I bought a DVD player from your shop last week. The first time I used it, it started well. But then the pictures suddenly disappeared, and the machine began to make a strange noise.
>
> I took the player back to the shop and I asked for a refund. The shop assistant told me he could only repair the DVD player.
>
> The DVD player you sold me was clearly faulty. I now demand you give me a full refund for the player.

• Write an email to Mr Prandrakash:
  • acknowledging his letter
  • apologising for the problem with the DVD player
  • inviting him to return to the shop, and telling him that he can have a refund
  • offering him a replacement DVD player as an alternative to a refund.
• **Write 60–80 words.**

11.1

Health and safety

VOCABULARY

Signs

1 Look at these health and safety signs. Where could you see these signs?

2 Which sign tells you the following?

1 about a danger or hazard
2 what you mustn't do
3 where to find help for minor injuries
4 what procedures to follow
5 what to do if you see a fire
6 what to do if there's a fire
7 where to go in an emergency
8 where you should leave the building if there's a fire

LISTENING

A factory tour

Learning Tip

Practise taking notes while you listen to an item on the Internet. This will help you to focus on what you are listening to. Then listen to the item again and check your notes.

3 🔘 11.1 A group of new employees is on a tour of a cement factory. Listen to the health and safety officer giving the tour and tick which areas the tour visits.

the production area   the warehouse   the laboratory   the main offices

4 Complete the company's health and safety rules with eight of the items in the box.

arrive   fire alarm   fire extinguishers   food and drink   hard hat
protective clothing   smoke   temperature   warehouse   waste material

1 You must always wear a _____ when you are moving around the plant.
2 You mustn't _____ anywhere.
3 You can't enter the production area if you aren't wearing _____.
4 The _____ must be kept clean and tidy.
5 Always put all _____ into the bins.
6 You can only consume _____ in the canteen.
7 You should come to the assembly point when you hear the _____.
8 Visitors must sign in when they _____ at the plant.

5 🔘 11.1 Listen to the health and safety officer again and check your answers to exercise 4.

Modal verbs: *must(n't)* and *(don't) have to*

+	You **must** wear a hard hat. We **have to** clock in	It is necessary.
–	You **mustn't** smoke.	It is not allowed.
–	We **don't have to** wear hard hats in the office.	It is not necessary.
?	**Must** we clock in?* **Do we have to** clock in? *have to* is much more common in questions	Asking if something is necessary.

Note that the past tense of *must* is *had to*.
We **had to** do a fire drill yesterday.

6 Use the modal verbs in the box to complete the sentences. Use each verb twice.

> must   mustn't   don't have to   had to

1 I _____ be late for work. My boss will be angry.
2 I had terrible toothache, so I _____ go to the dentist's after work yesterday.
3 I love the weekends. I _____ get up at 6.30 to go to work.
4 Sorry I'm late. I deleted my report by mistake and I _____ type it all again.
5 I _____ leave work on time tonight. I've missed the train home three times this week.
6 I _____ fall asleep at my desk after lunch again. Otherwise, I'll get the sack!
7 I _____ fly to Geneva every month now because we use video-conferencing.
8 I _____ deal with these invoices today. It's the last day of the month.

7 Work in pairs. Look at the picture and find ten hazards. Then choose the correct verbs to complete the list of health and safety rules for this workplace.

1 Women *should / must / shouldn't* wear high-heel shoes at work.
2 Stairs *can't / don't have to / must* be clear of obstacles.
3 All exits *don't have to / should / can't* be kept clear.
4 You *have to / can / mustn't* leave any objects on the floor.
5 You *should / mustn't / don't have to* behave correctly at work.
6 You *don't have to / must / shouldn't* tie back your hair if it is long.
7 You *have to / mustn't / can't* wear a protective mask when operating machines.
8 You *can / mustn't / should* smoke.
9 For safety reasons, you *don't have to / can / mustn't* wear a tie when operating machines.
10 When lifting boxes, you *don't have to / should / mustn't* bend your knees.

8 What rules or guidelines are there in your workplace? Compare with a partner and ask follow-up questions.

A: We have to wear white coats in the laboratory.
B: Oh, we don't have to wear any special clothing. Why do you have to wear white coats?

Why is it dangerous?

1 Which do you think is more dangerous – office work or air travel? Compare with your partner, giving reasons for your answer.

2 Work alone.

Student A: Read Text A.

Student B: Read Text B.

Answer the questions below.

1 What is DVT?

2 Who does it affect?

3 Why does it happen?

4 What can you do to prevent it?

Text A

Text B

NEWS

Thousands of office workers hospitalised every year with DVT

Hospitals are reporting increasing numbers of cases of DVT, or deep vein thrombosis, among office workers. DVT is a lump, or clot, in the blood, and it often forms in the veins in the legs. In a minority of cases, DVT causes death – up to 1,000 people died last year in the UK. DVT is not a new medical problem, but it is increasing because of the way we work these days. Office workers, especially people who work in IT or telephone call centres, spend most of the day sitting down and this allows clots to form. They can't get up and move around the office because they have to be in front of a computer screen to work. However, doctors say that DVT is easy to prevent. Walking around the office for a few minutes every hour, and doing simple exercises to move your legs and feet, can greatly reduce the risk of DVT. Doctors are recommending that all companies give guidelines to their office employees about preventing DVT.

NEWS

DVT risks for air travellers

DVT, or deep vein thrombosis, is not a new medical condition, but it is a symptom of modern lifestyles. DVT occurs when a person's blood forms a lump, or clot, and this can block the vein. It can have serious consequences, including death. About 1,000 people die in the UK every year from DVT. It is becoming more common because more people than ever before are flying around the world. Thousands of air travellers suffer from DVT every year, and the rate is increasing. Most people, when they get on a plane, sit down and then don't move from their seat during the flight. Sitting still in this way increases your risk of DVT enormously. The good news is that it's easy to prevent DVT. Simply wearing loose, comfortable clothes and moving around regularly during the flight is enough to reduce the risk. It's also a good idea to drink plenty of water and not alcohol and, when you're sitting in your seat, to do some exercises which move your feet and legs.

3 Work in pairs again. Ask your partner the questions in exercise 2. How do your partner's answers differ from yours?

4 Work in groups of three. What other health problems can result from sitting all day in an office environment? Write a list of recommendations and advice for an information pack for new employees. Mention parts of the body (eyes, back, hands and wrists, etc) as well as office conditions, such as noise, temperature and humidity.

You should take a break every hour.

In your break

5 Which of these activities do you do in your breaks at work/school? Tell your partner what you usually do.

read the newspaper	check your email	surf the Internet
go for a run	chat with colleagues	play video games
play table tennis	have a massage	have a shower
play the piano	have a snack	stand at the coffee machine

6 Read the article about the Googleplex, the main office of Google. Which of the activities in exercise 5 could you do at Googleplex?

Google™

GOOGLE'S HEADQUARTERS in Mountain View, California, is referred to as 'the **Google**plex'. The entrance lobby is decorated with a piano, lava lamps, old computers, and a projection of search queries on the wall. The hallways are full of exercise balls and bicycles, but these are not just for decoration; it isn't unusual to find them being used by **Google** employees who are taking a break from their computer screen to do some exercise. In fact, recreational amenities are found throughout the campus, and include a gymnastics room with weights and rowing machines, and locker rooms with showers and hair dryers. Employees also have the use of a massage room, assorted video games, a baby grand piano, a pool table and table tennis. In addition to the recreation room, there are snack rooms stocked with a huge variety of healthy foods. People can choose from various cereals, toffee, dried fruit and nuts, yoghurt, carrots, fresh fruit, and there are dozens of different drinks on offer, including fresh fruit juice and 'make your own' cappuccino.

Google co-founders Sergey Brin and Larry Page said, 'We think a lot about how to maintain our culture and the fun elements. We spent a lot of time getting our offices right. We think it's important to have a high density of people. We all share offices. We like this set of buildings because it's more like a densely packed university campus than a typical suburban office park.'

7 Would you like to work for a company like Google? Tell your partner why / why not. Use information from the text to explain your answer.

go, play and do

8 Complete the questions with the correct form of *go, play* or *do*. Then ask your partner the questions. Ask follow-up questions with *when, how often, where, who with,* etc.

1 Do you _____ football or any other team sports?
2 Do you _____ running?
3 Do you _____ to a gym regularly?
4 Have you ever _____ yoga?
5 Do you _____ some exercise every day?
6 Do you _____ skiing in the winter?
7 Have you ever _____ golf?
8 Would you like to _____ swimming in your lunch break?
9 Have you ever _____ rowing?
10 What other activities do you _____ to keep fit?

9 Write down as many activities and sports as you can in two minutes. Work in pairs for another minute and add any extra activities to your list. Which pair has the most activities? Write *go, play* or *do* next to each item.

11.2 Reporting accidents

GRAMMAR

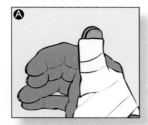
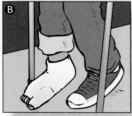

The past simple and past continuous

1 Match the explanations of the accidents (1–3) with the pictures (A–C).

1 He was talking on his mobile and he walked into a glass door.
2 He was opening a box and the knife slipped.
3 He was carrying a computer and he dropped it on his foot.

2 Underline the past simple verbs and circle the past continuous verbs in the sentences in exercise 1. Which action started first in each sentence?

> We use the past continuous with the past simple to talk about activities that were in progress when another action happened.
>
> Note that we can use *when* and *while* with the past continuous; we usually only use *when* with the past simple. We can use *when* and *while* either in the middle or at the beginning of a sentence.
> *He was opening a box **when** the knife slipped.*
> ***When/While** he was opening a box, the knife slipped.*

3 Write the past simple or past continuous form of the verbs.

1 She _____ (run) to answer the phone and she _____ (trip) over a wire.
2 I _____ (cross) the street and a car _____ (hit) me.
3 When I _____ (play) football, I _____ (twist) my ankle.
4 She _____ (get) out of the car and her scarf _____ (get) stuck in the door.
5 While he _____ (change) the cartridge, the ink _____ (spill) on his shirt.
6 We _____ (walk) to the car park when a tree _____ (fall) on top of a car.

4 Have you ever had an accident? Tell your partner what happened.

LISTENING

After the accident

5 🔊 11.2 Louise works at Maple plc. Last week she had an accident at work, but the accident report form was not completed correctly. Listen to the conversation between Louise and Ruth, from the quality department. Fill in parts A and B of the form with one or two words or numbers.

6 🔊 11.2 Listen to the conversation again and complete section C of the form.

A About the accident

date	(1) _____
time	(2) _____
place (inside/outside)	(3) _____
injury (state part of body injured)	(4) _____
first aid given (yes/no)	(5) _____

B About the injured person

full name	(6) Louise _____
department	New Accounts
number of days off work	(7) _____

C Brief description of accident (state if vehicles, machinery, etc involved)

(8)

7 Read the memo from the head of quality at Maple plc. What is the purpose of the memo?

   A to find out how healthy staff are

   B to find out if there are enough cupboards

   C to avoid any more accidents

From: Head of quality

To: All heads of department

May 12

Last week a member of staff suffered minor injuries after using a chair to reach a file on top of a cupboard. Please carry out the following checks in your department, in the next seven days, and report any action that needs to be taken.

   1 Assess the level of health and safety awareness of your staff.

   2 Review your filing and storage systems.

   3 Check the condition of office furniture and equipment.

Thanks, everyone.

Sheila

8 11.3 Annie and Sally work in the accounts department at Maple. Listen to their conversation in the office and choose the correct option (A–C).

   1 Sally has to

     A computerise the records.

     B sort the old records.

     C keep all the records.

   2 From now on, they

     A don't have to keep any of the files.

     B must keep files inside cupboards.

     C mustn't keep files on top of cupboards.

   3 Annie's office should buy

     A a set of ladders.

     B special stools.

     C new chairs.

   4 Annie has to

     A be back in the office at 2pm.

     B go to the maintenance department in the afternoon.

     C meet the maintenance man before lunch.

9 11.3 Listen to the conversation again. Decide which things they are doing are a result of the memo from the head of quality.

10 Imagine you are the head of the accounts department at Maple. Write a reply to the memo from the head of quality. State what action you have taken in your department on points 2 and 3 of her memo, and request some training on workplace risks for your staff. Write 30–40 words.

Theme park safety

1 Do you ever go to theme parks? Do you like going on rides? Why? / Why not?

2 Read this letter. How safe is Fantasy City?

24 January

Dear Fantasy City staff,

Congratulations to all staff and thank you for making Fantasy City theme park one of the most popular and the safest theme park in the country! Once again, we have the best safety record of all Theme parks. The recent safety inspection carried out by the Heath and Safety Executive has awarded us 'excellent' in all categories. Last year was our most successful year since we opened, and I want to continue that success in the coming year. In fact, I am sure we can do even better than we did last year. Our targets for this year will be decided soon, and I am confident that you will all do your best to achieve them.

Well done, everyone!

Kurt

Kurt Bayer
CEO
Fantasy City Theme Park

3 How do theme parks ensure the safety of their visitors? Compare ideas with your partner.

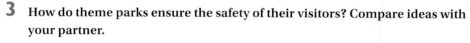

You have to be over a certain height to go on some rides.

4 Work in pairs. Look at some incidents (A–H) at Fantasy City and decide which descriptions (1–4) are most appropriate.

Incidents

A A girl fell on broken glass in the burger bar and cut her legs.

B A man suffered a heart attack on a roller coaster. It was his third heart attack.

C A child fell out of a ride that had a broken safety lock.

D A pregnant woman had to go to hospital after a ride on the Space Mission Simulator.

E On the hottest day of the year 257 people were treated for heat exhaustion and dehydration.

F A boy was taken to hospital after he choked on his chewing gum on a ride.

G A child who jumped into the aquarium was hit by a dolphin and suffered a bruised arm.

H A man fainted from fear at the top of the MegaTower ride.

Descriptions

1 pre-existing health condition in guest

2 responsibility of park

3 responsibility of guest

4 accident: nobody is considered responsible

Safety suggestions

5 Work in groups of four. You work for Fantasy City Theme park. Look at Kurt Bayer's safety suggestions for next year. Hold a meeting to discuss the suggestions and decide whether to accept or reject each one.

Student A: Chair the meeting.

Student B: Tell the meeting what current procedures are in each case. Look at page 128 for the information.

Students C and D: Keep a record of the decisions.

Useful language	
I think that's a good idea.	I'm not sure about this.
I think we should do that.	I disagree.
It's simple and effective.	We can't do that. It's too expensive.

SUGGESTIONS FOR NEXT YEAR	
LOST CHILDREN	Give children arm bands with radio microchip
QUEUE CONTROL	Use movable barriers at entrances to rides
SMOKING	Should be banned in the whole park
ALCOHOL	Mention that alcohol is banned on Guest information leaflet
TECHNICAL INSPECTIONS	Monthly external inspections
RIDE RESTRICTIONS	Designate all rides with min/max height – easier for public to understand
INFORMATION, SIGNS ON RIDES, ETC	Check and rewrite where necessary & update Guest information leaflet
GUEST INFORMATION LEAFLET	Make leaflet part of entry ticket – guests will have it at all times

Information leaflet

Exam Success

In the Writing Test, leave time to check your writing for spelling, grammar, vocabulary and punctuation mistakes.

6 Work in groups of four, in two pairs.

Students A and C: Write a new section for the Guest information leaflet to include instructions and advice, following your decisions at the meeting.

Students B and D: Write a memo to Kurt Bayer summarising your recommendations from the meeting.

7 In your group of four, form two new pairs. Read your partners' texts and check that the information is correct.

11.3

Listening Test: Part Four

EXAM FORMAT

APPROACH

In Part Four of the Listening Test, you have to listen to a conversation or interview, between two or more people, that lasts about three minutes. There is a table on page 34 which summarises the types of question in each part.

- Before the conversation, listen to the instructions.
- Understand what the conversation is about. What are the people discussing?
- After the instructions, you have 45 seconds before the conversation starts. Read the questions. Underline important words in the questions and answers. This will help you to hear the answers.
- As you listen to the conversation for the first time, listen for the words you have underlined. Listen also for synonyms of the words you have underlined. Try to choose the answers to the questions.
- As you listen to the conversation for the second time, either confirm your answers or change them.

1 There is a typical exam task from Part Four of the Listening Test on the opposite page. Read questions 1–8 and the options for each question. Work through the following steps with a partner before you listen to the recording.

1 Discuss what the listening text will be about. Make a list of ten other words you think you might hear.

2 Underline important words in the questions and answers.

3 Analyse what you will have to listen for in each question. Look at question 4. The correct option is the one you *don't* hear in that section of the conversation. Look at question 7. Say the numbers out loud.

4 Questions and options often use synonyms of the words you will hear. Write synonyms for the following words: *reduce* (question 5), *company employees* (question 6), and *all (companies)* (question 8).

2 11.4 Listen to the recording and answer the questions.

3 Compare your answers to questions 1–8 with your partner. Explain why you chose each option.

4 11.4 Listen again and check your answers.

PART FOUR

- You will hear a radio interview with Richard Orson, who introduced an environment-friendly policy into his company, Personal Touch.
- For each question 1–8, mark one letter (**A**, **B** or **C**) for the correct answer.
- You will hear the conversation twice.

1   When did Peter Walker start thinking about an environment-friendly policy?
   A after profits had suffered
   B after a meeting organised by the local business association
   C after giving some seminars

2   What did the environment-friendly policy involve?
   A careful planning of production procedures
   B spending some of the profits to change the business approach
   C reducing waste

3   How many visits did the assessment company make?
   A one
   B two
   C three

4   Which of the following was NOT mentioned in the first report?
   A heating and lighting
   B water and electricity consumption
   C recycling drinks cans.

5   By how much did the company reduce solid waste?
   A over 25%
   B over 30%
   C over 40%

6   How were company employees involved?
   A People were appointed to collect suggestions.
   B People were appointed to recycle drinks cans.
   C People were appointed to check computers and lights.

7   How much money does Personal Touch save every year?
   A £34,000
   B from £3,000 to £4,000
   C from £23,000 to £24,000

8   What kind of companies does Richard think that an environment-friendly policy could benefit?
   A all companies
   B only small companies like his
   C large companies

12.1

The job market

LISTENING   Job satisfaction

1   Work in pairs. Tell your partner what you like about your current job/position. Is there anything you don't like about it? What would you like to change?

2   🔘 12.1   Listen to an interviewer asking five people about job satisfaction. What do the people talk about? Write the interview number next to the topic.

salary	work colleagues	working from home
holidays	flexible hours	overtime
promotion	unemployment	responsibility at work

3   🔘 12.1   Listen to interviews 1–4 again. For each person, complete the notes using one or two words.

Reason for the change

Person 1   to save _____ and _____

Person 2   to have more time with _____

Person 3   to _____ for her hotel room

Person 4   to use his _____

4   Work in pairs. What other benefits are there from the changes the people would like to make? Think of two benefits for each person. Then compare your ideas with a new partner.

The second conditional

5 Read the sentences and underline the *if* clauses. Then answer the questions below.

1 I would keep in touch by email if I didn't go to the office every day.
2 If I worked flexitime, I would come to work earlier.
3 If I could go on holiday in June, the beaches wouldn't be so full of noisy children.

A Which form of the verb is used in the *if* clause?
B Do the sentences refer to events in the past or to imaginary/unlikely situations?
C Does a second conditional sentence always begin with *if*?
D Which sentences have a comma?

6 Match the beginnings of the sentences (1–6) with the endings (A–F) to make complete sentences.

1 If I took my holidays in September,   A if I worked at home.
2 If I worked flexitime,   B the beaches would be empty.
3 I would save money on petrol   C I would avoid the traffic.
4 If I earned more money,   D I wouldn't do the lottery every week.
5 I would make big changes   E I would be very unhappy.
6 If my work colleagues left the   F if my boss gave me more responsibility.
   department,

7 Complete these sentences using the correct form of the verb.

1 I'd really like that job. If I _____ (have) more experience,
   I _____ (apply) for it.
2 I've never been to China. If I _____ (can) speak Chinese,
   I _____ (look) for a job there.
3 He _____ (stay) until the end of the meeting if he
   _____ (not / have) a flight at 6pm this evening.
4 It's going to be difficult to get a visa. It _____ (be) easier if you
   _____ (have) a sponsor.
5 She's on a good salary here. She _____ (change) jobs if she
   _____ (want) more money.
6 An interpreter will be very expensive. If they _____ (speak)
   Russian, they _____ (not / need) one.

8 Put the verbs in the correct form and answer the questions for yourself. Then ask your partner.

1 What you / change about your current job? _____
2 If you / not work in this company, where you / work?
   _____
3 If you / can, / you / work from home? _____
4 What / be the advantages of working from home?
   _____
5 If you / can have any job, what it / be? _____
6 If you / lose your job, what you / do? _____

9 If you were the managing director of the company where you work, what would you do? Compare your ideas with two other students.

Working abroad

1 **Would you like to work in a different country? Tell your partner why / why not. Use these ideas and your own.**

a limited time	my family	married / single
no alternative	good pay	somewhere warm / cold
language	promotion	a new experience

A: I would work anywhere if it was only for a limited time – maybe six months. I think it could be an interesting experience.

B: I wouldn't like to leave my family at home. If I was single, I would consider it.

Migrant workers

2 **Read the article from a recruitment agency's website and choose the best title (A–C).**

A Businesses prefer migrant workers

B Exploitation of migrants continues

C New restrictions on migrant workers

A recent survey of UK businesses asked the question, 'What reasons do you have for employing migrant workers?' The answer was good news for EU citizens who want to come and work in the UK, and bad news for young British people looking for work. About 20 per cent of employers think that migrant workers are more productive and have a more positive attitude to work than British workers. In addition, 25 per cent of businesses can't find British workers with the necessary skills, and almost 20 per cent can't find people with the right experience. One hotel manager said, 'If I had to choose between a local person and an EU migrant, I would always choose the migrant worker. In my experience, they work harder and have better skills.'

The UK is a popular destination for skilled workers and graduates from countries like Poland and the Czech Republic. Many work in agriculture or the tourism industry, or in small businesses in the financial services and technology sectors. Some come to earn more money while others are looking for experience they can't get at home. Artur, from Poland, says, 'I work for an IT company and I would never get this level of experience at home. But I spent six months as a painter when I first arrived; if I repeated the experience, I would try to find a good job first.' Jakub, from the Czech Republic, said, 'I was sure I would find work quickly, and I did. The money is quite good, but if my English was better, I would have more opportunities for promotion. So now I'm studying again!'

Ralph Bowles, the director of an international PR agency, says, 'We have several European graduates working here, and I would happily employ more if they had the skills we need. We decided to hire graduates from outside Britain because it was difficult to find good UK people.'

3 **Read the article again. Decide whether these sentences are 'Right' or 'Wrong'. If there is not enough information to choose 'Right' or 'Wrong', choose 'Doesn't say'.**

1 The survey asked companies if they would employ migrant workers.

   A Right   B Wrong   C Doesn't say

2 Most employers think that migrant workers are better than British workers.

   A Right   B Wrong   C Doesn't say

3 About 20 per cent of companies employ migrant workers.

   A Right   B Wrong   C Doesn't say

4 The tourism industry is the most popular destination for Polish and Czech workers.

   A Right   B Wrong   C Doesn't say

5 Artur could not find a job in IT in Poland.

   A Right   B Wrong   C Doesn't say

6 Jakub found a job when he arrived in the UK.

   A Right   B Wrong   C Doesn't say

7 For Ralph Bowles, a graduate's skills are more important than his/her nationality.

   A Right   B Wrong   C Doesn't say

4 Compare your answers with a partner. For the questions that you have answered 'Right' or 'Wrong', which words helped you to decide the answer? For the questions you answered 'Doesn't say', why did you give this answer?

Getting a job

5 Read the advice from a website for migrant workers in the EU and complete the text with the correct words.

> application   CV   employers   interviews
> qualifications   recruitment   skills   vacancies

MOVERS AND WORKERS

If you want to arrange a job before you move, there are several websites especially for foreign workers where you can find lists of
(**1**) _____. Your (**2**) _____ and your
(**3**) _____ forms should be completed in the language of the country, not your own language. If you are already in the country, you should register with different (**4**) _____ agencies; this is often easier than contacting (**5**) _____ direct. They will want translations of your (**6**) _____. It's a good idea to do additional training courses to show that you are adapting your (**7**) _____ to the country you are in. In addition, several local colleges offer one-day courses to help foreign workers prepare for job (**8**) _____, open bank accounts, etc. Check with your nearest college to see what is available.

Problems at work

In Part Two of the Speaking Test, you have to comment on what the other candidate says. As your partner speaks, try to remember the main points he/she makes.

6 Work in pairs. Prepare a short presentation (one minute) on three problems people could have when working abroad and how to deal with them. Form new pairs and give your presentations.

7 Work in groups of three or four. Read the situations below. In your groups, discuss what you would do in each situation. Then form new groups and report what you would do.

1 You are in charge of the accounts department in a pharmaceutical company. You hear that the parent company plans to relocate your department to Hungary in the next 18 months. Some members of your staff have also heard the rumours.

2 You are the owner of a small language services company. A regular client has asked you to review your prices for translation services. Your client has asked another translation company for a quote. This company's prices are 15 per cent lower than yours.

3 You run a business making high-quality furniture to order. Your company has won a large export contract to supply furniture for a luxury cruise ship. Your production capacity is too small to fulfil the contract.

12.2

Job applications

An advertisement

1 Tell your partner about your first job. Explain what it was, how much you earned and how you got the job.

2 Read the job advertisement for a position in public relations and say which paragraphs give information about these areas.

A the company _____

B contact details _____

C the salary _____

D the position _____

E the candidate _____

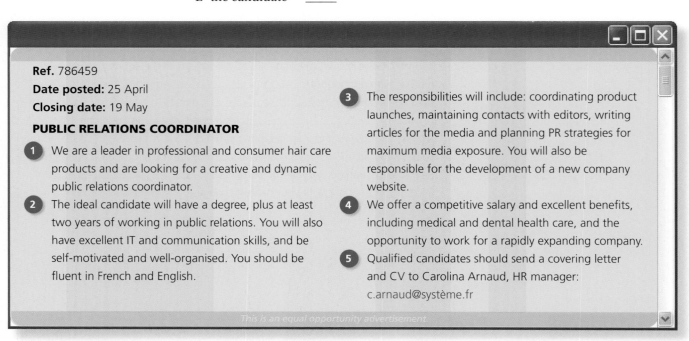

Ref. 786459

Date posted: 25 April

Closing date: 19 May

PUBLIC RELATIONS COORDINATOR

1 We are a leader in professional and consumer hair care products and are looking for a creative and dynamic public relations coordinator.

2 The ideal candidate will have a degree, plus at least two years of working in public relations. You will also have excellent IT and communication skills, and be self-motivated and well-organised. You should be fluent in French and English.

3 The responsibilities will include: coordinating product launches, maintaining contacts with editors, writing articles for the media and planning PR strategies for maximum media exposure. You will also be responsible for the development of a new company website.

4 We offer a competitive salary and excellent benefits, including medical and dental health care, and the opportunity to work for a rapidly expanding company.

5 Qualified candidates should send a covering letter and CV to Carolina Arnaud, HR manager: c.arnaud@système.fr

This is an equal opportunity advertisement.

Learning Tip

Read a wide variety of text types, including advertisements, lists, timetables, catalogues, etc. Try to identify the important information in each one.

3 Read the advertisement again and complete the notes.

Company name _____

Job title _____

Qualifications required _____

Experience required _____

Skills required:

• job-related skills _____

• languages _____

• personal qualities _____

How to apply _____

4 🔘 12.2 Listen to the conversation between Jenny and Maria, two PR assistants in a cosmetics company. Has Jenny got the qualifications, experience and skills required?

5 Do you think Jenny is a suitable candidate for the position? Why? / Why not?

A covering letter

6 Read these guidelines for writing a covering letter. Is anything missing?

A covering letter should
- give your contact details
- give the name and address of the person you are writing to
- state the reason for writing
- give brief details of qualifications and skills
- explain why you are the right person for the job
- explain why you want the job
- refer to attachments or enclosures, such as your CV
- use a formal style

7 Read the covering letter that Jenny sends to Système. Does it follow the guidelines in exercise 6?

Dear Ms Arnaud,

I am writing to apply for the post of public relations coordinator currently advertised on the Independent website (Ref. 786459).

I have worked in public relations for four years, since I completed my degree in French and German. *Currently, I am* a PR assistant with Gloss Cosmetics, *where I* am responsible for organising our participation in trade shows, as well as assisting in product launches.

I am creative and self-motivated, and *I enjoy* working with people. I am looking for a position with more responsibility, where I can use my language skills.

I attach my CV. If you require any additional information, please do not hesitate to contact me.

I look forward to hearing from you.

Yours sincerely
Jenny Hamilton
jhamilton@gloss.co.uk
(44) 610 739 433

8 What differences are there between a covering letter sent through the post and an emailed letter?

9 Choose one of the job advertisements on page 129, or find one online or in a newspaper. Write a covering letter to accompany your application form or CV. Use the sections in *italics* in the letter in exercise 7 as a guide.

10 Work in pairs and exchange your letters. Has your partner followed all the points in the guidelines in Exercise 6?

A job interview

1 Work in pairs. Read these questions from an interview for the post of marketing assistant. Decide if the interviewer (I) or the candidate (C) would ask each question.

1 What do you enjoy most about your current job?
2 How do you deal with difficult situations in your current job?
3 Where would I be based?
4 Why would you like to work here?
5 What responsibilities would I have?
6 What would you like to be doing in a few years' time?
7 How does your experience match this position?
8 Would I be able to use my language skills?
9 What qualities do you bring to this position?
10 What would you say were your weak points?
11 What kind of training would be available?
12 Could you tell me something about the pay and conditions?

2 Add two more questions to the list in exercise 1.

3 12.3 Listen to an interview and tick the questions you hear in the list above.

4 12.3 Listen to the interview again and choose the correct option (A–C).

1 What does Philip say about his current job?
  A He likes the variety.
  B He enjoys meeting lots of people.
  C He enjoys the routine.
2 What does he say about routine administrative tasks?
  A He doesn't do that kind of work.
  B He wouldn't like to do an administrative job.
  C He thinks they are important.
3 Why would he like to work for the company?
  A He wants to earn more money.
  B He wants more responsibility.
  C He doesn't want to work for a big company.
4 What would he like to do in the future?
  A He'd like to manage his own team.
  B He'd like to run his own business.
  C He'd like to stay with the company.
5 What qualities does he offer?
  A He is creative and competitive.
  B He is well-qualified and knowledgeable.
  C He is determined and motivated.
6 What are his weak points?
  A He doesn't have any.
  B He isn't always patient.
  C He doesn't like impatient people.

5 Would you give Philip the job of marketing assistant? Why? / Why not?

6 Work in groups of four, in two pairs. Choose a job that one of you does, or a job that you would like to do.

Pair A: Work together to prepare interview questions. Use ideas from exercise 1.

Pair B: Prepare for the interview using ideas from exercise 4 to help you.

7 In your group of four, form two new pairs. Carry out the interviews. Is the candidate successful?

WRITING

Interview follow-up

8 Look at the Useful language box. Read the beginnings of sentences from a letter following a job interview. Which ones could be used in a letter offering someone a job? Which could be used in a letter turning down a candidate?

> **Useful language**
>
> I am writing ...
> I am pleased to inform you that ...
> I regret to tell you that ...
> We would like you to ...
> Please confirm ...
> We will keep your details ...
> We look forward to ...
> We wish you luck in your ....

9 In pairs, write suitable endings for the sentences in the Useful language box.

10 Do you think Philip got the job? If you think he did, write an email to Philip telling him:

- that his application was successful
- the date the company would like him to start work
- that he should reply by email to confirm his acceptance of the position offered

If you think Philip didn't get the job, write him an email:

- thanking him for attending the interview
- telling him that his application was not successful
- informing him that you'll keep his CV in your files

12.3

Reading Test: Part Six

EXAM FORMAT

In Part Six of the Reading Test, you have to choose the correct answer from three options to complete twelve spaces. In this part of the exam, the focus is on grammar. You will need to look closely at the structure of the text. This type of test is called a cloze test.

APPROACH

- First, read the text to get an idea of what it says.
- During the first reading, don't look at the options, but try to predict which words go into the spaces.
- Next, read the text again. Underline the words before and after each space.
- Think about the type of word/words that could go in the space.
- Next, look at the options. If one of them is the same as, or similar to the word/words you thought of, it is probably the correct answer. Make a choice, and write the word/words in pencil in the space.
- When you have written something in every space, read the whole text again.

EXAM PRACTICE

Here is a typical task from Part Six of the Reading Test. Read the instructions and do the task.

PART SIX

- Read the Business Book Review below.
- Choose the correct word (**A**, **B** or **C**) to fill each gap.

A business book review

As technology brings people (**1**) ..... together, our environment becomes more varied. And while workers (**2**) ..... all backgrounds are merging into the global marketplace, businesses (**3**) ..... being challenged by a lack of skilled and qualified employees who can integrate successfully into other cultures.

(**4**) ..... the book *Diversity: Leaders Not Labels*, author Stedman Graham points out that we (**5**) ..... become a member of anyone else's culture in order to play a key role, but we must maintain our (**6**) ..... identities while respecting others' uniqueness in our workforce and in our (**7**) ..... . The people who (**8**) ..... succeed in the 21st century are those who do not look at a person's race, who build relationships, who continue to (**9**) ..... and develop (**10**) ..... individuals, and who (**11**) ..... value to (**12**) ..... and those they represent.

	A	**B**	**C**
1	more close	closer	the most close
2	from	in	on
3	is	are	were
4	For	In	On
5	must not to	do not have to	do not have
6	own	owe	owed
7	community's	communitys'	communities
8	will	won't	don't
9	grow	grew	grown
10	like	such as	as
11	brought	bring	brings
12	them	themselves	their

Reading Test: Part Seven

In Part Seven of the Reading Test, you have to read two short texts and complete a form using information from these texts. You will need to extract relevant information and complete a form accurately.

- First, read the form in order to understand what information you have to look for in the letter and memo.
- Next, read the letter and the memo carefully.
- Look at the first item on the form. Look for the answer in both texts.
- On a separate piece of paper, write down all the possible answers.
- Choose the correct answer from the possible answers. Remember to write in CAPITAL LETTERS.
- Look at the next piece of information on the form.

Exam Success

- Don't spend too long on one question. Leave it and go to the next question.
- When you have done all of the parts, go back to the difficult questions.
- Don't leave any questions unanswered.
- Check that your writing is legible.
- Remember to transfer all your answers to the Answer Sheet.

2 **Here is a typical exam task from Part Seven of the Reading Test. Read the instructions and do the task.**

PART SEVEN

1 Read part of a letter and the memo below.

2 Complete the form.

3 Write a word or phrase (in CAPITAL LETTERS) or a number on lines **1–5**.

Following our telephone conversation this afternoon, I confirm that, because of serious illness, Maureen Chant will be unable to attend the personnel management course beginning on Monday 17 June. I would therefore like a refund for the cost of the course. The enrolment No. is PM/173D

McGuire's Institute of Business

Memorandum

To:	James
From:	Linda
Date:	5 June
Subject:	Refund

Please fill in the refund form for the client. NB The course starts on 19 June, and the enrolment No. is PM1/173D. The sum to be refunded is $770.

McGuire's Institute of Business

Refund number 064

Enrolment number:
(1) ....

Participant's name:
(2) ....

Course:
Personnel management

Starting date of course:
(3) ....

Reason for refund:
(4) ....

Refund due:
(5) ....

How to approach the BEC Exam

Paper One: Reading and Writing

- Organise your time: in the Reading and Writing Test, you have 1 hour 30 minutes, so leave some time to answer every part.
- There is no fixed time for answering each part. In the Reading Test, remember some parts contain longer texts (Parts Four, Five and Six), so you may need more time for these than others. Remember also that Part Six contains twelve questions and is worth more marks than the other parts.
- Do not leave any question unanswered. If you are not sure of an answer, choose what you think is the most likely answer. If it is wrong, you will not be penalised; but if the answer is correct, you will get one more mark.
- In the Writing Test, Part Two is worth twice as many marks as Part One, so it is a good idea to leave more time for Part Two than for Part One.
- In both Part One and Part Two, include all of the points in the question.
- In both the Reading and the Writing Tests, you must use a pencil to write your answers. If you need to change your answer, you can use an eraser.
- You may make notes on the question paper, but you must only write your answers on the Answer Sheet.

Paper Two: Listening

- Before the recording is played for the first time, read the instructions and task carefully. Think about what you are going to hear and underline any important words in the questions.
- At the end of the test, you will have ten minutes to transfer your answers to your Answer Sheet. Answer all questions. If you are not sure of an answer, choose what you think is the most likely answer. If it is wrong, you will not be penalised.
- Use a pencil to write your answers. If you need to change your answer, you can use an eraser.
- The first time you listen, you should try and understand the general meaning; the second time, you should listen for the details.
- The first time you listen, don't spend too long thinking about an answer. If you are not sure, leave it until you listen the second time.

Paper Three: Speaking

- Listen carefully to the instructions given by the examiner and try to understand them. If you don't understand the instructions, you may ask the examiner to repeat them.
- Speak clearly and loudly enough for the examiners to hear you.
- Avoid using long sentences and leaving long pauses.
- Listen carefully to the other candidate when he/she is talking, and respond to him/her.
- Allow the other candidate to answer. Do not interrupt him/her and do not dominate the discussion.
- If you don't know a word or phrase, try to explain it using other words.
- Try to use correct vocabulary and grammar. But if you make a mistake, don't worry too much. If possible, correct any mistakes you make.
- Don't give one-word answers. Be prepared to explain your answers, to start a discussion and to develop the ideas of the other candidate.

MODULE 7

Page 71, Exercise 9 Making an order

Student A: You are the office manager of Inflatable World Ltd. Give the caller (Student B) information about the following items.

Article Number	4832-CA (inflatable castle)
Size (metres)	Length: 5.5 Width: 5.5 Height: 5.5
Weight (kilograms)	140 kg
Prices (euros)	4-hour rental: €220 8-hour rental: €260 2-day rental: €340

Article Number	685–SL (inflatable slide)
Size (metres)	Length: 20 Width: 4.5 Height: 6
Weight (kilograms)	450 kg
Prices (euros)	4-hour rental: not available 8-hour rental: €280 2-day rental: €360

MODULE 8

Page 83, Exercise 4 We've got a problem

Student A: First, listen to Student B's problem and make suggestions. Use the expressions from exercise 2. Then choose one of the problems below and explain the problem to Student B. Use the expressions from exercise 2.

1 Your office manager has left without giving notice. It is the end of the month and there is a lot of paperwork to deal with.

2 Your warehouse keeps being broken into. You think it could be vandals. Nothing of great value is stolen, but it is expensive to repair doors and windows repeatedly.

3 Your main supplier has gone out of business. It is your busy season and your order books are full.

Page 50, Exercise 3 In-company communications

Student B: You are Octavio Flores, head of the design office. Your office has been very busy and only two of the three designs are ready. The third design should be ready tomorrow afternoon. You are going on holiday tonight. Answer the call from Elena Gonzalez.

Page 113, Exercise 5 Safety suggestions

Student B

	CURRENT PROCEDURES
Lost children	They are taken to Guest Services
Queue control	No special procedure
Smoking	Allowed in designated areas
Alcohol	Not allowed
Technical inspections	Daily by on-site technicians, quarterly by external engineers
Ride restrictions	Some rides have 1.4m height restriction
Information, signs on rides, etc	No special procedure
Guest information leaflet	Too many people don't read it

Page 99, Exercise 7 Don't just manage, lead!

If you have scored between 10 and 25, you probably aren't comfortable as a leader. You prefer roles which contribute to the success of the team, but without taking all the responsibility. You are probably good at generating ideas or supporting your colleagues, and your team values your input.

If you have scored between 26 and 45, you show that you have potential as a leader. You probably already have some experience of taking responsibility and directing others, and you are quite successful at this. Perhaps now is the time to decide how to perfect your leadership skills.

If you have scored between 46 and 50, you definitely want to be the leader – all the time and in every situation! Remember, other people can also make valuable contributions! Perhaps now is the time to analyse your leadership style and reflect on how you achieve your results.

Page 102, Exercise 5 Small talk

1 FALSE. On first meetings or more formal occasions, people in the UK use 'Mr/Mrs/Ms' + surname. Otherwise, they use first names, but they never say 'Mr Peter'.
2 FALSE. Formal dress is a suit, but smart–casual clothes are acceptable in many offices. Some companies have a policy of allowing more casual dress on Fridays.
3 FALSE. Personal gift-giving isn't part of UK business culture, although corporate hospitality is common in big companies.
4 TRUE. In a UK business context, people are expected to arrive at the time specified, and not to leave early.
5 FALSE. These topics are normally taboo, and so is religion. People in the UK like small talk to be neutral, so the weather, travel, the family and home countries are all acceptable.
6 TRUE. Handshakes are usually quite firm – because this suggests commitment and respect.

Page 121, Exercise 9 A covering letter

TRAVEL SALES ADVISOR

We are looking for a Travel Sales Advisor to join our team in our busy city centre office. We are one of the biggest travel companies in the UK and can offer excellent conditions and career prospects.

You will be dealing with customers face-to-face and by telephone, offering the full range of our holiday packages and services.

You will have excellent communication skills and be attentive to customers' individual needs. You will have several years' experience in the travel industry, and will be comfortable working under pressure.

Applications, with a covering letter, should be sent to the Human Resources Manager. Click here to download the application form and full contact details.

ACCOUNTS CLERK

NRC is an international courier service based in Brussels. We are looking for an Accounts Clerk to join our busy team in our main office.

The successful candidate will have a strong background in accounting and good IT skills. Training in our in-house accounting systems will be given. You will be reliable and show attention to detail. You will be able to work independently and meet deadlines.

Responsibilities will also include contact with foreign clients. An additional foreign language is highly desirable.
We offer a generous salary and benefits package.
For further details and an application form, click here.

Introducing and talking about yourself

Greetings

Good morning. / Good afternoon. / Good evening.
Hello. / Hi.
Goodbye / Bye.
Have a nice …
See you … / on …

Introductions

May I introduce myself?
My name's …
Call me …
Pleased to meet you.
How do you do?
How are you?
Not too bad, thanks.
Nice to see you again.
This is …
What's your name?
How do you spell that / your name?
I'm a …
I work for …

Talking about jobs and work

What do you do? / What's your job?
Who do you work for? / Do you work for … ?
Do you like your job?
What does your job involve?
Are you responsible for … ?
Are you in charge of … ?
Who deals with … ?

Expressions for communication

Arranging a meeting

When can we meet?
Can we meet on … ?
How about …day?
Are you free on …day?
What are you doing on …day?
How does … sound?
That sounds good.
Sorry, I can't. I'm busy at / on … I'm …
We could …

Using the phone

Can I help you?
Who's calling, please?
I'm sorry, the line is busy.
I'm afraid … is not in her office at the moment.
Would you like to leave a message?
Can I say that back to you?
Does she have your number?
I'll ask … to call you when she gets back.
I'll pass your message on to … .
This is … , of …
I'd like to speak to … , please.
Can I leave him a message?
I'll call back later.
I'll give it to you.

Making reservations

I'd like to book …
I'm afraid the … is fully booked.
Is there a … still available?
Would you like to make a booking?
Can I have the … name, please?
The booking is for …
Could you send … to confirm the booking?

Talking about problems

Is something wrong?
Is it serious?
What's wrong (exactly)?
I'll contact … immediately.
I'll sort it out as soon as I can.
I'm sure we'll find a solution.
Could you tell … (as well), please?

Making invitations

Would you like to … ?
Yes, I'd be delighted.
It's very kind of you (to ask, but …).
Thanks, that sounds great.
We're thinking of … Are you free?
Good idea, what time shall we meet?
Yes, I'd like to join you.
Thanks, but …
Can I offer you … ?
I'm afraid I don't …
Yes, please.
A glass/cup of … , please.
Have you tried the … ?
I'm sorry, I …
I think I prefer …

Brainstorming

The first thing we have to do is …
When we know …
Let's …
Can we … ?
You'll have to …
I'll …

Expressions for the Speaking Test

Answering personal questions

I'm a …
I'm / I come from …
It's a … / It's in / near …
I live in / with …
I work in / for …
I study … / at …
I've lived / worked / studied there for … / since …
At the moment, I'm studying / working …
I'd like to work (for / in / as) …
I'm interested in …
I like …
I've got …

Asking the examiner to repeat a question

Sorry, could you repeat that, please?
Sorry, can you say that again?

Giving your mini-presentation

I think the most / least important thing is … (because …)
I think … is more / less important than …
I don't think … is important.
… is important too.

Agreeing/Disagreeing and discussing with your partner

What do you think?
I think …
So do I. / Do you? I don't.
I don't think …
Neither do I. / Don't you? I do.
Do you agree?
I (don't) agree (with you).
I (don't) think so.
You're right.
I see what you mean.
I'm not sure.

Expressions for correspondence

Informal and neutral writing

Hi / Hello, Best wishes / regards (email)
Dear John, Best wishes / regards (letter)

Formal letters

Dear Mr (Brown), Yours sincerely
Dear Sir/Madam, Yours faithfully

Making invitations

I am writing to invite you …
We would be delighted if you could …
I enclose details of …
Please confirm …
Thank you for …
We can confirm …
I confirm our …
We will be delighted to …
It will be a pleasure to …
I'm very sorry, but …
I regret that …

Dealing with complaints

I apologise for …
Please accept my apologies for …
I would like to apologise for …
Unfortunately, …
The problem was due to …
We had a problem with …
I would like to offer …
I can offer …
Please accept …

Applying for a job

I am writing to apply for the post of … which is advertised on … website / which was advertised in the …
I have worked as … / in … / for … / since …
I attach my CV. If you require any additional information, please do not hesitate to contact me.
I look forward to hearing from you.

Module 1

 1.1 What does your job involve? *(page 7)*

Janet Good morning, everyone. I'd like to welcome you all to this session about public speaking. My name's Janet Coyte, and I'll be your trainer for today and tomorrow. I can see your names and the companies you work for on your badges, but I'd like you to say something about your jobs and responsibilities. Katherine, would you like to start?

Katherine Certainly. Hi, I'm Katherine Alessi and I work for Marfil Solutions. I'm a management consultant. Marfil Solutions gives companies advice on their markets, organisation and processes. I interview clients, identify problems and suggest solutions.

Mark Morning. My name's Mark Jenkins. I'm a sales rep for Soap Heaven. I visit customers and leave product samples. I look for new customers, and I support my company's customer service department.

Kostas Hello, I'm Kostas Hadavas. I'm the personal assistant to the managing director of a company called Athens Daily Menu, which provides catering services. I arrange the MD's travel and accommodation for business trips, I organise his meetings, and I deal with correspondence.

Suzanne Good morning. My name's Suzanne Wilkes. I'm the chief financial officer of a company, P&B Europe, which designs gadgets and gifts. I'm responsible for the company's accounts, I advise the managing director on financial matters, and I control the money that comes in and goes out.

Carmen Hello, I'm Carmen Selles. I'm the quality manager in a company that produces car seats and interiors. I arrange and carry out tests of our products and I deal with customers' complaints. Oh, the name of the company is CarSpek.

 1.2 *(page 10)*

I = Ian   **H** = Henry   **S** = Sarah

I Hello. May I introduce myself? My name's Ian and I work in the Asia–Pacific division.

H Nice to meet you, Ian. My name's Henry and this is my colleague, Sarah.

S Hello, Ian. Do you work in the Sydney office?

I No, not at the moment. My boss is in Sydney. But I'm based in Singapore.

H Look! There's Michelle over there. She's based somewhere in Asia. I can't remember where exactly. Do you know her?

I Yes, we're on the same project this year. She's in Singapore, too.

H Ah, lucky you. She's really beautiful – and clever too.

I Yes, I know. It's a real pleasure to work with her.

S Well, I think I'll leave you boys to discuss ... work.

H Oh, Sarah, you're not jealous, are you?

S No, I'm not ... Michelle, how lovely it is to see you again.

1.3 *(page 12)*

I = Interviewer   **K** = Kostas

I What's your name?

K Kostas Hadavas.

I How do you spell your surname?

K H–A–D–A–V–A–S.

I What do you do?

K I'm the personal assistant to the managing director of Athens Daily Menu.

I Who's the managing director?

K His name's Georgos Solomos.

I What does your job involve?

K I deal with clients, and I organise meetings and events.

I Do you write reports too?

K Yes, I often write reports and memos for our staff.

I Do you work only in the Athens area?

K No, we don't. We work in other parts of Greece too.

I How do people react to you, a man, doing this job?

K Sometimes they are surprised, but it isn't usually a problem at all.

I Do you like your job?

K Yes, I like it a lot.

I Why do you like it?

K Because I'm always busy, and because of the variety of things I do.

Module 2

 2.1 New projects *(page 16)*

V = Vicky   **S** = Steve

V Hello.

S Hi, Vicky.

V Hi, darling. How are things in Brazil?

S Pretty good. And with you?

V Fine. Where are you calling from?

S My hotel in Fortaleza. It's on the north-east coast.

V Is it nice there?

S Yes, the scenery is amazing.

V And what are you doing in Fortaleza?

S I'm working on the plans for the shopping centre. What are you doing right now?

V Oh, it's sunny today, so I'm working in the garden.

S And what are the children doing?

V They're watching TV. No, that's not right. Tommy's playing on his computer, and Emma's with her friends, I think.

S Good. And are you doing anything nice this weekend ...

 2.2 Arranging a meeting *(page 20)*

D = Dave   **M** = Martina

D Dave Prakash.

M Hi Dave, it's Martina. Listen, I need to discuss the designs for the new R300 series with you. When can we meet?

D I can't make it today, I've got meetings all day. How about Monday morning?

M I'm visiting the new plant on Monday morning, but the afternoon is OK.

D I'm probably taking time off in the afternoon, actually.

M OK. Let me see ... are you free on Thursday?

D No, I'm visiting clients on Thursday morning, and then I'm flying to Prague on Thursday afternoon.

M Are you going to the trade fair?

D Yes, that's on Friday morning. I'm coming back on Friday afternoon. Look, what about Tuesday, for lunch?

M No, I'm meeting the sales team on Tuesday and it's an all-day thing. That leaves Wednesday.

D Wednesday looks OK at the moment, but don't forget the strategy meeting at 10 o'clock.

M Oh, that's right, I'm going to that too. But I'm free after that. How does 12.30 sound? We could have lunch.

D Great, we can talk and eat on Wednesday. Now I must run. I've got a meeting with the Finance Director.

2.3 *(page 23)*

B = Bob   **F** = Felix

B Felix, are we planning to go to the New Directions Book Fair this year?

F Yes, I think so. It's always a good event. We usually make lots of new contacts. When is it?

B It's in June this year. It's on Thursday and Friday the 21st and 22nd.

F Oh, just a second. Aren't we going to Helsinki that week?

B No, the Helsinki conference is in July.

F Oh yes, that's right. Fine, let's go to the Book Fair.

B There's a special reception on the 21st.

F Is it at lunchtime?

B No, it's in the evening at 8 o'clock.

F Sounds great! Can you get everything organised?

B No problem. I'll confirm our attendance.

Module 3

 3.1 *(page 28)*

Our guest today on 'Songs of my life' is the entrepreneur Martha Lane Fox, of the massively successful company lastminute.com. With her business partner, Brent Hoberman, Martha Lane Fox started lastminute.com in Brent's living room. The idea was simple – a website selling late flights and late hotel bookings. The company grew very quickly and expanded from the UK into France, Germany and Sweden. They bought other travel companies, and after six years they had 1,400 employees. Lastminute.com went public in 2000, and the shares in the company increased their value by 40 per cent in two days. Martha Lane Fox left the company in 2003. True to her entrepreneurial spirit, she wanted to start more new companies. Martha, it's a pleasure to have you here in the studio …

 3.2 Company structure *(page 31)*

Parker Electronix is based in Fleet, in the south of England. We are leaders in hardware and software solutions for satellite technology. My uncle, John Parker, founded the company in the 1960s. Our latest product is a new program for optical instruments for the European Space Agency. Our engineers are involved in all of the stages of a project, from planning to the final performance validation. The industrial department, supervised by Gerhard Kulzer, provides regular certified training for its staff. The R&D activities, supervised by Ross Benton, are essential for all future applications. We have a workforce of 60 employees and a turnover of $7.5 million. Now, let me introduce Arnaud Gamage, our contracts & purchasing manager. Arnaud will explain to you …

3.3 *(page 32)*

… and now I would like to turn to the final section of the report. As you can see, last year was an excellent year in production. The first two quarters were rather slow, but as a result of new orders from Asia, our production rose dramatically in the third and fourth quarter. This situation was reflected, of course, in our sales for last year. We started the year in a strong position, but in the second quarter worldwide sales fell sharply. This was a result of the high price of oil. However, as I mentioned earlier, new orders from Asia meant that sales went up to their previous level by the end of the year. Looking now at the share price, I am delighted to announce that last year was also an excellent year in this respect. The share price rose steadily for the first two quarters, and it remained steady at its maximum for the rest of the year. All in all, last year was a very positive year …

 3.4 Exam spotlight, Listening Test Part One
(page 35)

1

M Hello, Janet. Did you send those letters to our Italian suppliers?

F Yes, I sent them on 13 June. Let me check … No, sorry. I sent them on the 14th.

M Great, thanks.

2

M1 The new management have decided to invest in staff training.

M2 Oh, really? I knew nothing about that. What do they want us to do?

M1 They want us to improve our performance when presenting and negotiating, and make the most of our computer skills. Somebody has complained that our computers are out of date and so are our skills!

M1 Yes, I think they're right. Personally, I need to work on how to prepare my presentations.

M1 Me too. Let's start with presentation skills, then.

3

This is the answering machine for Benton Factory Outlet. We are open Monday to Wednesday from 9.00am to 6.15pm. On Thursday and Friday we are open from 9.00am to 7.15pm. We are closed on Saturday and Sunday.

4

F1 Here are the P&W logos the agency has just sent.

F2 Mm, let me see … I like the colours …

F1 What about the shapes?

F2 I'm not very keen on squares or rectangles.

F1 So, do you prefer this one?

F2 Yes, the circle is nice.

5

M1 Our booking for the Magic Children Expo has been confirmed.

M2 Excellent! Now we have to organise the stand. By the way, where exactly is the stand?

M1 Let me have a look. I've got the fax here. It's number 18 in Hall J.

M2 Ah, that's the same hall as last year.

M1 Yes, but last year our stand was number 80.

6

M1 The exhibition went better than last year.

M2 Yeah, I'm really glad. It was a great success – especially for us.

M1 There were more people than last year. I've got the figures – yes, 15,312. That's a lot more than last year.

7

The sales were very good in December. Then we saw the usual decrease in January and February, and we recovered a bit in March.

8

F Hello, this is Jane Howell from Conference Room number 4.

M How can I help you, Ms Howell?

F We asked for 120 bottles of water, one for each delegate at our meeting, but there are only 100. Could you send us 20 more?

M Do you prefer sparkling or still water?

F Still, please.

M I'll send them to you immediately.

F Thanks a lot. Bye.

M Bye.

Module 4

 4.1 Views on import controls *(page 37)*

Presenter The crisis over clothing imports is still hitting the headlines, and we spoke to some of the people involved. In

Portugal, Joao da Silva owns a small factory in Aveiro.

Joao Look, I can't see any problem with these import controls. The European Union should protect European industry – people like me and my factory workers. We can't produce clothing at the prices the Chinese charge. I employ a small number of people, it's true, but they depend on me. Where else could they work around here? My message to Mr Mandelson is this: stop the Chinese imports, support European producers.

Presenter But it's a different message from the retail clothing chain *Tulip*. Listen to what Dagmar Rasmussen has to say.

Dagmar We in the retail trade really think we should import garments from China, or from Malaysia, or from any country that can supply us at a good price. Why should the European Union tell us where and how to do business? We are not at all happy with this situation. Our shops could be almost completely empty next week. What are we going to say to our customers? The European Trade Commissioner should act at once, and permit the clothes to leave the warehouses and to stock our shops. Really, this can't go on!

 4.2 Views on import controls (*page 37*)

Newsreader 1 And now for the business news from Susan Fleming.

Newsreader 2 Today's headline is that China and the European Union have just announced that an end to the clothing blockade has been agreed. Millions of fashion items are sitting in ports around Europe, where they have been since import restrictions were introduced in June. Today, however, both sides in the dispute have reached an agreement, and the clothes will be in the shops soon. The EU will accept all of the 80 million items. However, only 50 per cent of these items are part of this year's imports. The other 50 per cent will be part of next year's import quotas. China agreed to this solution, which is a compromise on both sides. The agreement is a victory for Peter Mandelson, the EU trade commissioner.

Newsreader 1 And on the stock exchange …

 4.3 (*page 40*)

R = Receptionist   **C** = Customer

R Wates' Office Supplies Ltd, can I help you?

C Hello, I'd like to speak to Mariah Keaton, please?

R Who's calling, please?

C This is Jane Barrett, of Bryant & Sons.

R I'm afraid Ms Keaton is not in her office at the moment. Would you like to leave a message?

C Yes, I would. Our order has arrived, and you've sent the wrong items. We ordered three boxes of A4 paper, five printer cartridges, two boxes of pencils, and four boxes of pens. You sent us two boxes of A5 paper, the wrong printer cartridges, only one box of pencils, and no pens.

R I see. Which printer cartridges did you order?

C The code is HP92274A.

R And which did you receive?

C The code on the ones we received is FO26ND.

R OK, Ms Barrett, I'll ask Ms Keaton to call you when she gets back. Does she have your number?

C I think so. But I'll give it to you all the same. It's 0573 764812.

R Can I say that back to you? 0573 764812.

C That's right.

R I'll pass your message on to Ms Keaton.

C Thank you. Goodbye.

 4.4 (*page 42*)

N = Natalia   **S** = Sven

N Westlaine Pharmaceuticals.

S Hello. I'd like to speak to Natalia Marin, please.

N Speaking.

S Hi, Natalia. It's Sven. I need your budget figures for the report. Can you email them to me?

N They're not ready yet, I'm afraid. I'd like to check them again. Some of the figures aren't quite right.

S When do you think they'll be ready?

N I'm working on them now. I'll send them to you this afternoon. Is four o'clock alright?

S Yes, that's fine. I'll write the report tomorrow morning.

N Oh, by the way, Margareta is leaving next week. We're having a little party tomorrow afternoon. Would you like to come?

S Yes, I'd love to. What time?

N Half past three.

S Great. I'll see you tomorrow. Bye.

 4.5 Telephone messages (*page 43*)

1

M Good morning. Could I speak to Mr Aitken, please?

F I'm afraid he's not in the office today. Can I take a message?

M Just tell him Cailin called.

F Could you spell your name, please?

M Sure, it's C–A–I–L–I–N.

F Thanks so much.

2

F And your address is?

M 27, Mendip Road.

F 27, Pendip Road.

M No, M for Madrid. Mendip.

3

M Hi, Sue. Can you call me back on 98 983 988?

F Let me just check that – 98 983 988?

M Yes. Can you call me back right now, please?

4

F And when is the delivery due?

M On the 23rd.

F Did you say the 21st?

M Sorry?

F Do you mean the 21st, 2–1, or the 23rd, 2–3?

M Oh I see. The 23rd, 2–3. The 23rd of June.

4.6 Telephone messages (*page 43*)

1

R = Receptionist   **C** = Customer

R Reid, Whelan and Blake.

C Hello, I'd like to speak to Ms Chandra.

R I'm afraid she's not in today. Can I take a message?

C Yes, this is Joe Panetta, from AS Associates.

R I'm sorry, Panetta … is that P–A–N–E–double T–A?

C Yes, that's right.

R And you're from AS …

C … Associates.

R Thank you. So what's the message, Mr Panetta?

C I'm calling about the brochure Ms Chandra wanted. Can you tell her that our new brochure is coming out in two weeks' time? Would she like to wait for that one rather than receive the old one now?

R I'm sorry, did you say two days or two weeks?

C Two weeks. Could you ask Ms Chandra to phone me and confirm which one she wants?

R Yes, of course. Does she have your number?

C I'll give it to you. It's 0632 158431.

R Alright, Mr Panetta, I'll pass your message on to Ms Chandra.

C Thanks.

R You're welcome. Bye.

2

R Reid, Whelan and Blake.

C Hello, can I speak to Mr Horbaczewski?

R I'm afraid he's off sick. Would you like to leave a message?

C Yes, my name is Bob Davis.

R Could you spell your surname, please?

C Sure. D-A-V-I-S.

R And what is the message?

C I need a copy of my tax form for last year. Could you ask Mr Horbaczewski to email a copy to me, please?

R Certainly. Does he have your email address?

C I'm not sure. I'll give it to you anyway. It's B D dot Davis, at hotmail dot com.

R All right, Mr Davis. I'll give your message to Mr Horbaczewski.

C Thank you very much.

R Not at all. Goodbye.

3

R Reid, Whelan and Blake.

C Hello, is Maria Peters in today?

R She is, yes, but she's in a meeting at the moment. Can I take a message?

C Yes, this is Sigrid Junge, from Hofmann GmbH.

R I'm sorry, could you spell your name, please?

C Alright. Sigrid S-I-G-R-I-D, Junge J-U-N-G-E.

R And what was the name of the company?

C Hofmann, that's H-O-F-M-A-N-N, G-M-B-H.

R Thank you. Now what is the message?

C I can't fly to London on 17 April. There are no places available. But I can come on the 18th. Could you ask Maria to confirm that she can see me on the 18th?

R Yes, of course. Does she have your number?

C Yes, she does.

R All right, Ms Junge, I'll give your message to Mrs Peters.

C Thanks.

R You're welcome. Goodbye.

4

R Reid, Whelan and Blake.

C Hello, I'd like to speak to Mr Dando.

R His line's engaged. Would you like to wait?

C Yes, please. ...

R Hello, caller. I'm afraid the line is still busy.

C Can I leave message?

R Certainly. What is the message?

C Could you tell him that I have accepted the first offer?

R You've accepted the first offer. OK. And could you give me your name, please?

C Oh, yes, of course. Martin Kraemer. That's K-R-A-E-M-E-R.

R Thank you. I'll give Mr Dando your message.

C Thank you.

4.7 Telephone messages *(page 43)*

1

Gabrielle Hello, Roberto? It's Gabrielle. Can you tell me when the goods are arriving?

Roberto Well, they're leaving on 16 February, and the journey takes three days. If everything goes well, you'll have them on the 19th.

2

Personnel officer Good afternoon, Personnel.

Caller Oh, please excuse me, I think I must have the wrong extension. I wanted to speak to the production manager. Could you tell me her extension number, please?

Personnel officer Certainly, it's 2319. But she's not in her office at the moment. She's having a lunch meeting with the managing director.

3

Krystof Krystof Grivas's office. I can't come to the phone at the moment. Please leave a message, and I'll get back to you as soon as I can.

Berndt Yeah, Krystof, it's Berndt. The time is now one o'clock. Look, I won't be able to make our 2.30 meeting. Can we make it a bit later – 4.30 perhaps?

4.8 Exam spotlight, Speaking Test Part One
(page 45)

E = Examiner   **C1** = Candidate 1   **C2** = Candidate 2

E Good afternoon.

C1 and C2 Good afternoon.

E My name's Heather Barras and this is my colleague, Sharon Hutchinson. She will be listening to us. Now, could I have your mark sheets, please?

C1 Yes, here you are.

C2 Here you are.

E Thank you. Right. So, what's your name?

C1 My name is Christine Benferrhat.

E How do you spell your surname?

C1 It's B-E-N-F-E-R-R-H-A-T.

E And where are you from, Christine?

C1 I'm from Brittany, in France.

E And what's your name?

C2 My name's Joao Cordeiro and I'm from Portugal.

E Joao, do you work or study in Portugal?

C2 I work for an advertising company and I attend evening classes in English.

E And you, Christine, do you work or study in Brittany?

C1 I finished school last year. I have a new job near Paris. I work for a multinational company.

E And do you like your new job?

C1 Yes, I like it a lot. I like speaking English with my colleagues and our customers.

E And what about you, Joao? Do you like your work?

C2 Yes, I like it very much. I like working with creative people.

E OK. Christine, what do you do in your spare time?

C1 I don't have much spare time, but I like reading, listening to the music and I like swimming. When I go back to Brittany, I also like windsurfing.

E And you, Joao, do you have any hobbies?

C2 Yes, I like taking photos. I have a new digital camera and I like taking pictures of towns. I also like going to the cinema and I visit art exhibitions. There are a lot in Lisbon.

E Do you think it's better to live in a small town or a big city?

C2 I prefer big cities. It's exciting and there's a lot to do.

E Do you agree, Christine?

C1 No, I don't agree with him. I live near Paris, but that's because of my work. I would prefer to live in a smaller town, like my home town in Brittany. Maybe because I like the sea.

E Thank you. That's the end of Part One of the Speaking Test.

Module 5

5.1 Career changes *(page 49)*

P = Petra   **A** = Alex

P Excuse me. Could you pass me a plate?

A Sure. ... You're Petra Schein, aren't you?

P Yes, I am.

A I thought so. You probably won't remember me, but I came for an interview for an accountancy job with you about three years ago.

P Yes, Alex, isn't it? Bélanger.

A That's right.

P I seem to remember that one of your hobbies was photography. It was a real passion.

A You do have a good memory!

P So what happened? We offered you a job, but you went to work for one of our competitors – Deutsche Bank, I seem to remember.

A The conditions they gave me were better, I'm sorry to say.

P I can understand that. So, are you still working there?

A No, I've given up banking altogether. I worked for Deutsche Bank for a little more than two years, but I didn't really like the job. There was too much competition among the employees, and I didn't really like that.

P Well, sometimes you have to be competitive if you want to make progress.

A I know, but it wasn't for me.

P So, what do you do now?

A I have become a professional photographer.

P You know, that doesn't surprise me. Are you in any particular sector?

A I take portrait photos. I've just bought a studio, and I'm creating a library of photos, which I'm going to publish on my website.

P You must give me your web address.

A Better than that, I can give you my business card. ... And what about you? Are you still in human resources?

P Yes, I am. I've moved to the head office, and I'm the manager there. So now I'm even busier than ever ...

 5.2 *(page 51)*

F = Franka   **B** = Berndt

F Hello. It's nice to see you again. You're looking well.

B Thanks! I am well. I've just come back from the Turin Book Fair.

F Ah! One of your favourite events. How did it go?

B Oh, the fair was quite a success. We had a lot of interest in a new series of science titles that we've published. And I met up with some old friends. Do you remember Nuno, from Lisbon? Yes, all in all, it was very pleasant. And I do enjoy Italian food.

F It's delicious, isn't it? Well then, Berndt, has this been a good year for you?

B Yes, it has. We've done really well in Western Europe – we've sold more books than ever before. And we've started distributing in countries in Eastern Europe as well – for example, in Poland and Hungary. Poland is doing very well. The demand for our books has been almost as high as in Spain and Portugal.

F That's great! I can see you've been very busy.

B Well, of course! You know me.

F So what's next then? I'm sure you've got something new planned.

B Well, we're going to move the actual printing to Slovakia. We have a new contract with a printing company in Bratislava. They're going to take over about 80 per cent of our book printing next year. It's going to cut our costs considerably, I hope.

F What a coincidence! I've just been to Bratislava.

B Well, I'm going to be there next month. I'm going to discuss the contract with the printers. And after that, I think I'm going to take a few days' holiday. It's been a very busy year.

 5.3 Negotiating a bank loan *(page 53)*

BM = Bank Manager   JH = Jack Hopkins

BM OK, well, I've got all the paperwork here for your loan application. Everything seems to be in order. Let's just have a look at your business plan. Perhaps you could tell me about your ideas?

JH Yes, of course. We plan to make fruit drinks, from 100 per cent fruit – no extra sugar, or additives or "E" numbers. At the moment, we've only got a couple of flavours, strawberry and pear, but we want to expand our range to include more flavours.

BM You say that you've got some flavours. Have you already started making and selling your drinks?

JH Only on a small scale, but they're selling really well and we can't keep up with demand.

BM Right, so why exactly do you want a loan? Are you going to expand your range or increase your production?

JH Well, both, we hope.

BM And how do you plan to sell the drinks? Direct to the public?

JH No, we're going to sell through other companies. You know, in cafés, snack bars, at outlets in airports and railway stations. We've already had talks with the catering company that runs the 'Travel Snack' chain. They're going to stock our drinks in their main outlets.

BM And are you going to be able to expand quickly?

JH I think so, because we're going to keep everything simple. We plan to use the same basic plastic bottles that we've used until now, and we're going to use fruit that is easily available locally. Our production process is very simple too.

BM OK, what about your market? Who do you think is going to be your main market?

JH So far most of our customers have been young people – you know, students, teenagers, people who are interested in drinking something healthy and natural. So we're going to try to consolidate that market. I don't think it's a good idea to change our strategy at the moment.

BM What kind of marketing have you done?

JH A friend of ours has designed a great website for us, and I think we're going to focus on the Internet for the moment.

BM OK, so let's look at these figures in more detail ...

Module 6

 6.1 Flight problems *(page 56)*

1

We got to the airport 30 minutes before the plane was due to take off, and we went straight to the check-in desk. First, the man at the desk said that the plane was already full because the flight was overbooked, so we couldn't get on.

But then he changed his story. He said there were empty seats on the plane, but we were late and the check-in desk was closed. So we missed our plane and we had to buy two tickets for another flight. You see, if the flight is overbooked, they give you a seat on a later one – but if you arrive late, you lose your money. I bet the man at the desk was lying.

2

I called the airline to ask if my flight was on time, and the man said that there might be a delay because of the snow. But when I arrived at the airport, there were no flights. The woman at the information desk told me to go back to my hotel and wait. She said they were going to close the airport, and she didn't know for how long.

3

I couldn't complain about anything. The airline sent a taxi to collect me from my hotel. At the airport, they took me straight to the desk to check my case in. I didn't have to wait. Then they let me sit in the First Class Lounge, even though I didn't have a first class ticket. The woman in the lounge said she would bring me some food from the buffet if I was hungry. Then, when it was time to go, they pushed my wheelchair all the way to my seat on the plane. And during the flight, they couldn't do enough for me.

4

There's one every week. If it's not the baggage handlers, it's the flight attendants, or even the pilots. The last time I travelled, it was the air traffic controllers. Oh, but they weren't stopping for the whole day, just for four hours, just long enough to cause absolute chaos. The announcement said there would be no cancellations that day, only delays. But that meant that I missed my connecting flight in Frankfurt and had to fly out to Chile the following day.

 6.2 At the hotel (*page 61*)

1

R = Receptionist   **G** = Guest

R Good afternoon. Carlton Hotel. How may I help you?

G Yes, hello. I'm phoning to check if my online booking went through. I haven't received any confirmation.

R When did you make your booking?

G Last Tuesday, the 14th.

R Could I have your name, please?

G Yes, it's Johanson.

R Let me see. Yes, Mr Johanson, we have a booking for you for Thursday, the 23rd, for one night.

G Good. Thank you.

2

P = Porter   **G** = Guest

P Can I help you with your luggage, Madam?

G Yes, please. I've got some very heavy suitcases. They're over there, on the right.

P Here you are, Madam. Which is your room?

G I'm sorry, these two big suitcases aren't mine. And this small one isn't mine either.

P They were the only suitcases on the right.

G Oh, I meant to say 'on the left'. One big suitcase and two small ones. I'm terribly sorry.

P No problem, Madam.

3

G = Guest   **C** = Chambermaid

G Who's there?

C It's Alice, the chambermaid. … Good morning, Sir. May I clean your room now?

G Yes, of course. I'm going out now. Er … the reception desk said I could give you my laundry. Is that right?

C Yes, that's right. Just leave your laundry in this bag.

G I need this pair of trousers cleaned. I'd like to wear them this evening. Do you think they will be ready by then?

C I'm sure we can manage that, Sir. What time this evening?

G I'll need them before eight o'clock.

C That's no problem.

G Thank you very much.

4

W = Waiter   **G** = Guest

W Are you ready to order, Sir?

G No, I just can't decide. What would you recommend?

W Well, would you prefer meat or fish?

G I don't really want meat or fish today. I'd like some vegetables.

W Then maybe you would like to try our dish of the day. It's made with local organic vegetables.

G Yes, that sounds nice. And a glass of red wine, please.

5

S = Secretary   **CS** = Conference speaker

S Hello. Business Centre. This is Christine speaking. How may I help you?

CS I'm in the main conference room and I've got a bit of a problem.

S What is the problem exactly?

CS Well, I've connected my computer to the video projector, and the Internet also seems to be working, but at this speed I won't be able to give my presentation. I need a faster connection.

S I'll call the technician, Madam.

CS Thank you. And ask him to come immediately. I'm getting nervous.

S I'll get him to come as soon as possible.

 6.3 Arranging business travel (*page 62*)

1

The next train to depart from platform six is the seven fifty-five to Manchester.

2

The eight fifteen Glasgow to London coach is now ready for boarding. Please make your way to the coach immediately.

3

Network Southwest apologises for the late arrival of the Bristol Express. This train will now arrive at twenty-three fifteen.

4

Due to a baggage handlers' dispute, all remaining flights today have been cancelled. There will be no flights until oh seven hundred hours tomorrow morning.

 6.4 Arranging business travel (*page 62*)

TA = Travel agent   **J** = Judith

TA Good morning. Langton Travel. Can I help you?

J Good morning. Yes. I'd like to book a flight to Paris Charles de Gaulle Airport, from London Heathrow, for tomorrow night.

TA For how many people?

J One adult. I see there's an Air France flight at 20.15.

TA Let me see, 20.15. Here we are, flight AF2271 … I'm afraid the flight is fully booked … but I see that there are still places on the six o'clock flight.

J No, that's too early.

TA Well, there's a British Airways flight at 19.40.

J No, that's also too early. I wanted a flight after 8pm.

TA Well, the British Airways flight is fully booked anyway. I'm afraid the Air France flight is the only one after eight o'clock.

J What about Wednesday morning? He needs to land at Charles de Gaulle by 9am.

TA Both Air France and British Airways have flights arriving at, or before, 9am. The BA flight leaves at 6.20 and arrives at 8.25, whereas the Air France flight leaves later but gets there at 9am exactly. Do you have any preference?

J Well, the British Airways flight gives him more time. Is there a seat still available on that one?

TA Yes, there is a seat available. Would you like to make a booking?

J Yes, please.

TA Can I have the passenger's name, please?

J Yes, it's Mr Michael, M–I–C–H–A–E–L, Burnett, B–U–R–N–E–double–T.

TA Do you have an account with us?

J Yes, the account code is LTBC 1784.

TA Thank you. OK, the booking is for one passenger on British Airways flight BA395 at 06.20.

J Let me take a note of that. Flight BA395, at 06.20.

TA That's right.

J Could you send an email to confirm the booking? My name is Judith Baird. You've got the address.

TA Yes, of course, Ms Baird.

J Thanks. Bye.

Module 7

 7.1 Hotels of the future (*page 68*)

I = Interviewer   **A** = Aisha

I Good evening. On this week's *Business Unusual*, I'm talking to Aisha Ghadir, the chief executive officer of Hydro Palace Hotels. Now, Ms Ghadir, from the name of your company, we can clearly understand that you are in the hotel business. But I believe there is something rather special about Hydro Palace Hotels.

A Well, we provide a luxury service for an exclusive clientele. But what is unusual about our hotels is the fact that they're underwater.

I When you say 'underwater', I assume you mean on the coast or at the water's edge?

A No, our hotels really are underwater – a true submarine holiday experience!

I Indeed! And not for the average family holiday budget, I suspect.

A Well, the hotels are not cheap to build, and maintenance and running costs are higher than for hotels on land. So, of course, if we want to make money, we have to charge more than normal hotels.

I So, how much does it cost to stay in one of your hotels?

A Well, let's consider the Anemone, which we opened two years ago in Florida, in the USA. One night costs $940 per person. There are 20 double rooms, so the hotel can accommodate up to a maximum of 40 guests.

I I see. I understand you've just opened a new hotel in Fiji.

A Yes, that's right, the Nautilus opened a month ago. One night there costs $1360 per person. There are 78 double rooms, so the hotel can accommodate up to 156 guests. And there's a theatre with live shows every night.

I The hotels are both underwater. But exactly how far down are they?

A Well, the Anemone is 10 metres below the surface of the water, and the Nautilus is 14 metres below.

I And how much did the hotels cost to build?

A The Anemone cost $47 million and the Nautilus $190 million.

I And your next hotel? Where is that going to be?

A In Dubai. Building started 18 months ago. It's going to open early next year. This is a larger project than the other two; the Atlantis will have 160 double rooms, and it will be at a depth of 23 metres below the surface. The cost of construction is estimated at $520 million.

I So, how much will a night in the Atlantis cost?

A We expect to charge about $1900 per person per night.

I Well, that does indeed sound like a very exclusive hotel. Thank you for coming to talk to us.

7.2 Making an order (*page 71*)

SA = Shop assistant   **C** = Customer

SA Good morning, Office Design. How can I help you?

C Hello. I want to buy a filing cabinet that will fit under my desk.

SA I see. And how high is your desk?

C It's 74 centimetres.

SA That's very good. We've got two filing cabinets, the FC12W and the FC12M, which are both 74 centimetres high.

C No, no, they're too big. You see, it's 74 centimetres to the top of the desk. The filing cabinet can't be more than 69 centimetres high.

SA I'm sorry, we don't have anything that small.

C I see. Well how big is the FC12W?

SA I'm sorry?

C The FC12W. What are the dimensions?

SA Oh, yes. Er ... well, as I said, it's 74 centimetres high, 50 centimetres wide, and 65 centimetres deep.

C That's 74 by 50 by 65. I see. And what about the FC12M?

SA It's the same size. The difference is that the FC12W is made of

wood, and the FC12M is made of metal. W for wood, M for metal.

C I see. So you haven't got one in plastic?

SA Er ... no. Only wood and metal.

C How many drawers have these cabinets got?

SA They've both got two drawers.

C I see. I wanted three drawers.

SA Well, these filing cabinets have only got two.

C I see. And how much do they cost?

SA The wooden cabinet costs £140. The metal one is cheaper at £90.

C And what colours do they come in?

SA The FC12W comes in a red wood finish, the FC12M in blue, black or grey paint.

C I see. No green, I suppose?

SA No, no green. You can always paint it if you want.

C Well, if I bought one FC12M, would you give me a discount because of the colour?

SA No, I'm afraid not. So do you want to buy one of the cabinets?

C Well, 74 centimetres is still too high, so they won't fit under my desk.

7.3 Changing ISP (*page 73*)

RM = Recorded message   **D** = Dana   **C** = Customer

RM Welcome to Maroon Communications. If you are an existing customer, press 1. For information about mobile phones, press 2. For information about our Internet services, press 3. For information about our small business packages, press 4. For all other services, please hold.

D Good morning. Business services department, Dana speaking.

C Hello, I'd like some information about the small business packages you have.

D Certainly, Sir. Can I just ask you some questions?

C Yes, of course.

D Are you self-employed or do you have a business?

C I run a small company.

D Does your company have fewer than ten employees?

C Yes, it does.

D And which services are you interested in?

C Well, I need mobiles for my staff of six and an Internet connection for the office, basically.

D We have a special offer at the moment for small businesses. It's called MaroonBusinessOne and it gives you unlimited national calls on both mobiles and landlines, a 24-hour broadband connection, and no charge for connecting calls.

C And how many mobiles does that cover?

D The cost of the phones themselves is separate, but the MaroonBusinessOne service covers up to ten mobile phone lines.

C What about support and maintenance?

D With the MaroonBusinessOne package, all calls to the technical support line are free.

C No, sorry. I mean if there are problems with the phones themselves.

D The package is a service contract, so the equipment itself is not covered. We do guarantee the broadband connection 24 hours a day, however.

C And can I have more than one computer connected?

D The broadband connection is to your computer network or to a single computer. It doesn't matter which you have.

C OK, that's good. And how much does this package cost?

D The monthly charge is 75 euros for the first three months, on special offer, and then 120 euros after that.

C Right. And how long does the contract last?

D There is a penalty charge if you cancel the contract before two years.

C Well, I want to think about this.

D Certainly, Sir. And don't forget that you can find all of these details on our website.

C Yes, good idea. OK, thanks very much.

D Thank you for calling. Please stay on the line to answer our customer services feedback …

 7.4 Exam spotlight, Listening Test Part Two

(page 74)

R = Receptionist **C** = Customer

R Good morning, Webster Training. Can I help you?

C Yes, hello. I'd like to make a booking for one of your computer skills courses.

R Certainly, Sir. Which one are you interested in?

C Well, from your brochure, it's Course ECDL12M.

R Parts 1 and 2 of the European Computer Driving Licence, right?

C Yes, that's right.

R And when would you like to do the course?

C At the beginning of September, if that's possible.

R I'm afraid the first week of September is already booked. But I have spaces available on the course starting on Tuesday the 9th.

C That would be fine.

R And how many people are hoping to attend the course?

C There'll be eight in total.

R I'm afraid we can take a maximum of only six people per group.

C I see. Well, six then. We might have another group later on.

R That's fine. And what's the name of the company?

C Coxten Ltd. That's C–O–X–T–E–N.

R And are you the person I should call if I have any information or questions?

C Yes. My name's Charles Goff.

R G–O–U–G–H?

C No, it's G–O–double–F. And my telephone number is 01536 848497.

R All right, Mr. Goff. Thank you for your booking …

 7.5 Exam spotlight, Listening Test Part Three

(page 75)

All right. Hello everyone. It's nice to see so many people. I'd like to welcome you this morning to this presentation of the company, Platt & Sons Ltd. My name is Barbara Platt, and I'm the managing director. Now, as most of you will know, we manufacture exercise equipment. We have a full range, all made to the highest standards. I'd like to say a little about how we began. The company was started in 1958, by my grandfather, Eugene Platt, who used to cycle competitively. Unfortunately, an accident put an end to his cycling career. That's when he started this company. He started off by producing bikes. The bikes he made in 1958 were competition models, but he soon started producing bicycles for recreational use. In the early 1970s, we brought out our first cycling machine, which was very popular with the general public, and a bit later on, we developed a range of these machines.

In the 1980s, we started producing other equipment, such as rowing machines and multi-gyms. With these, we saw our clients change from mainly private individuals, who wanted equipment for home fitness, to organisations like sports centres, which now account for about 60 per cent of our sales. We also sell to a lot of hotels.

We've recently started working with a sports doctor to design some machines specifically for use in hospitals. We expect to bring these new products out in the early spring.

So far, we've focused on the domestic market, here in Britain, but we intend to start exporting, first to other countries in the European Union. France and Germany are possible candidates.

And last, but certainly not least, you might have seen the recent reports in the local press. You might have read that Platt & Sons is suffering financial difficulties, because we lost an important contract to one of our competitors. I can assure you that there is no truth in the reports. Of course, we were sorry to lose the contract, but we are healthier than we have ever been.

Module 8

 8.1 Solving problems *(page 80)*

Good morning. We're continuing the theme of Total Quality Management this morning, and in this lecture I'm going to look at the concept of the Poka-Yoke mechanism.

Let's think firstly about things going wrong – about mistakes, in other words. Mistakes happen in organisations for many reasons, but we need to realise that almost all of them can be prevented. The secret, really, is people making the effort to identify when problems happen and to do something about them. This is where the use of poka-yoke mechanisms can prevent a mistake from becoming a catastrophe.

Let me illustrate with some everyday examples that you probably haven't thought about before. How many of you have ever filled up your car with diesel instead of petrol? I can see you shaking your heads, of course. You are thinking that the tube for the diesel is too big to fit into your petrol tank, which is correct. The tube is designed so that it only fits the right tank. So that's an example of poka-yoke, and it's a very simple idea. But what about putting the narrow petrol tube into your diesel car? Another poka-yoke mechanism, which actually measures the diameter of the tube, keeps the opening to the diesel tank closed in this case.

Staying with transport … A friend of mine once had a terrible experience when she tried to get off a crowded bus. The driver closed the doors without checking, and drove off! These days, modern buses use optical cells, like the ones you see in lift doors. These optical cells stop the doors from closing when people are getting off the bus.

Poka-yoke devices don't have to be high-tech though. What about those big stones you see on a rope on gates in the countryside? You don't need to worry about closing the gate behind you: the stone is used to make the gate close automatically.

Now, let's move back to organisations and the kinds of mistakes that can be prevented in the production process …

 8.2 *(page 82)*

A = Angela **D** = David

A Hi, David. Is something wrong?

D Yes, I think we've got a problem with our Txoko-cake line.

A Is it serious?

D Yes, I'm afraid it is.

A Oh, what's wrong exactly?

D Some kind of bacteria has been found in one of the machines.

A Oh no! Have you stopped production?

D Yes, of course. We're trying to find the cause of the problem right now.

A OK, I'll contact Head Office immediately.

D Could you tell the laboratory as well, please? They could help us.

A Yes, I'll do that too.

Module 9

9.1 A strategy meeting *(page 89)*

S1 = Speaker 1   **S2** = Speaker 2

S1 OK, so now that we've looked at the political, economic, social and technological analyses, I'd like to briefly complete the analysis by looking at the legal and environmental aspects.

S2 Yes, I imagine the legal situation is very complex.

S1 Well, you know, the legal factors were not so complicated until recently. The problem is that things are changing all the time in China. You know they recently changed the law on private property, and nobody can really predict what those changes are going to mean. So the whole thing is very difficult to comment on. It's a very unpredictable situation.

S2 I see. Well, I think we will need to look at that in more detail. I'm a bit worried about the implications there. And what about the environmental considerations?

S1 Well, obviously we need to do an Environmental Impact Assessment. The Chinese government are strict about corporate social responsibility, especially for joint ventures. So we will need to give them assurances and guarantees that we will stay within the emission targets. On the other hand, the areas where we could build plants are not environmentally protected, so that isn't going to be a problem initially.

S2 Great, something positive at last. By the way, what's the Chinese position with regard to the Kyoto protocol?

9.2 Crisis meeting *(page 90)*

L = Ludovica   **D** = Davide   **M** = Mirko

L This is the fourth emergency meeting today. Is there anything that's not an emergency in this company?

D Look, I'm sorry about this, but it's a real problem. I just got a call from Marek, and …

M Who is Marek?

L He's our Polish plant manager.

D … and they've been hit by a hurricane.

M In Poland? I didn't know they had hurricanes in Poland!

D No, I know. Anyway, the roof has blown off, and the electricity and telephones are down. Marek was calling from his mobile, but he said it took hours to get through and the communication was pretty bad!

M Was anybody hurt?

D Apparently not. But the workers on the night shift were evacuated.

L Any damage to the machinery?

D I have no idea. Marek sounded pretty worried. It will take some time to assess the damage.

M No electricity or phones – so, no Internet. They're completely cut off.

L They do have a generator. If it works, we can at least turn the system on.

D Wait, let's set priorities: the first thing we have to do is to limit the loss of production. Can we move production to one of our other plants?

L I'll check with the planning department.

D Good! Then they'll need somebody to help them with damage assessment – they don't have the experience for this. Ludovica, I'm afraid you'll have to help them. Call Marek on his mobile. Then send Jonathan over there as soon as possible.

L When we know what happened exactly, I'll send a small team to start the repair work and to coordinate the local maintenance people.

D Excellent! Now, the Internet … Mirko, what can we do until the electricity and telephone lines are repaired?

M Well, if they have a couple of mobile phones with computer connections, they will be able to connect up to the Internet.

L Then they can send us the production data we haven't got yet, and we can send them a couple of emails.

D Great! Let's get started.

9.3 Crisis strategy *(page 92)*

A = Announcer   **E** = Ellis

A Welcome to our Monday podcast for 5 March. Today our guest speaker is Ellis Whims, a PR expert, and she's going to talk about crisis management. Ellis over to you.

E A business crisis can take many forms. Unhappy customers can, unfortunately, give a lot of trouble. Do you remember the recent headlines about the woman who said she found a human finger in her food at a MegaBurger restaurant? MegaBurger estimate that this situation cost them $2.5 million in lost sales. And the story of the finger was actually false!

So if the unthinkable happens to you and your company, what do you do? How do you respond? Every organisation needs a crisis plan to enable it to handle a crisis quickly and effectively.

The most important part of crisis management is preventing a crisis in the first place. Take a hard look at your company and examine potential problems. An experienced public relations professional will help you to create your Crisis Communications Plan. This contains four steps:

First, collect information about the situation – make sure you know the relevant facts.

Second, appoint a Crisis Team – these people will be responsible for handling the crisis itself.

Third, appoint a spokesperson – this person will typically serve as the point of contact between your Crisis Team and the media.

Fourth, identify your key audiences – your customers, employees, salespeople, and the media.

If the worst should happen, don't panic. Take a deep breath and collect your Crisis Team. Examine the situation quickly and decide on the appropriate action, as well as the message you want to send to your customers, your employees, and the public in general.

The most important actions in a crisis are: acting quickly to resolve the situation, telling the truth, being available for the press, showing confidence and compassion, communicating changes in the situation as quickly as you can.

You've probably seen that when a customer experiences a problem and you resolve it for them quickly, that customer becomes more loyal than they were before the problem. The same phenomenon is true in a crisis. Communicating quickly and effectively to your key audiences can actually strengthen your brand image in their eyes.

A Thank you, Ellis. Thanks for listening, podcasters. Don't miss our talk next week, same day, same time.

Module 10

10.1 Creativity and leadership *(page 98)*

Good morning, everyone. Today's workshop will be in two sessions. In the second session of the workshop, you'll be trying out some tasks which are specifically related to some of the most common situations in today's business environment – and I think you'll see how they can help you to find creative solutions to everyday problems. We'll move on to the second session of the workshop after the break.

But in the first session of the workshop I want to look at some very easy things which you can do – things which you can do without any real effort at all – which will help to open up your mind, and make it easy for you to think in new ways. Scientists believe that doing activities to improve your memory and making small changes to your daily routine can actually make you cleverer, more confident and better at making decisions.

I'm going to give you a list of ten activities, and I want you to choose seven of them, which will give you a full week of activities. Then I want you to allocate one activity to each day of the week. Is that clear?

 10.2 Creativity and leadership (page 98)

So, let's get on with the list, then. As you can see, number one is 'have a shower' – nothing very unusual there – but I want you to have a shower with your eyes closed. Yes, try keeping your eyes closed while you're having your shower. And then, number two – 'brush your teeth' – you are going to do this with your other hand. So, if you are right-handed, you change to your left hand, and vice versa. Number three: you need to change your normal route to work and find a new way to get there. And at work, you can do number four, which is to choose some new words from a dictionary and use them in conversations. Number five on the list is something you can do in your lunch break or perhaps after work, as it's to go to a yoga or a meditation class. In fact, I think there are some yoga and meditation groups here in this centre. The next two items are real brain exercises; number six is to write your weekly shopping list and then memorise it and throw the paper away. And number seven is to do the Sudoku or, if you prefer, the crossword puzzle in your daily newspaper. Do you buy a daily paper? No? Well, I'm sure you can borrow one from a colleague! Or perhaps from someone you don't know – because item number eight is to talk to a stranger. So there you have a perfect opportunity to do that. And that brings us to our last two items on the list – both of them are to do with keeping your body healthy, because that's an important thing to remember. When we are tired or ill, our brains just don't work as well as usual, do they? It's difficult to be creative and innovative when we've got flu, isn't it? So, item nine, eat fish, like tuna or salmon, for your main meal. And finally, number ten is simple: no caffeine and no alcohol.

OK, so that's the list of ten activities. Now you decide which seven you will do and which days you will do them on. Next week we'll see how …

 10.3 What's still to do? (page 100)

B = Burton   **T** = Tracey

B Tracey, can you bring me up-to-date on how the Dublin Enterprise conference is going?

T Yes, everything is going well and there are only a few things to be finalised. The theme, as you know, is starting up and networking for small businesses, and we are aiming it at local business people.

B So it's basically an opportunity for businesses to get together and see what they can offer each other.

T Yes, that's one way of looking at it. We're hoping that it will strengthen the connections between local entrepreneurs, and help to create and develop new ventures.

B Have we confirmed the date as May the 4th?

T Yes, the dates are confirmed, but actually it's May the 3rd and 4th. It's a two-day event, running continuously from half past nine until half past five both days.

B And it's at the City Conference Centre again?

T Yes, everything is booked there. We've got the main room and four smaller rooms.

B Do we have a copy of the programme ready to go to print?

T Well, that's one of the things which I mentioned which still needs to be finalised. All the workshop leaders are in place, but we have a slight problem with the keynote speaker. Our original speaker has cancelled and we are still in the process of choosing an alternative speaker.

B I wonder, do we really need a speaker at an event like this?

T I think we do. It provides a focus to the whole two days, and last year's talk was a huge success.

B So, that needs to be finalised as soon as possible, doesn't it?

T Yes, it's the first thing on my list for after this meeting, don't worry!

B OK, what else?

T Well, again sticking with things which worked well last year, we're doing online enrolment via the website, and the event is being promoted on our website and all our associate websites, as well as in the press.

B Are we repeating the lunch? We had that Michelin chef last time, didn't we?

T No, I think that was for the Marketing Week, wasn't it? We're using the Conference Centre facilities, and providing hot and cold snacks all through the day.

B Well, it sounds as if it's all under control. Shall we leave it there for now?

T Actually, there was one last point. We're having some problems with the budget. The Conference Centre fees have gone up quite a lot since last year and that means we're having to try and make cuts in other areas. I'll have to ask Michelle to look at the figures again …

 10.4 The conference budget (page 101)

M = Michelle   **T** = Tracey

M I still think we're going to be over budget.

T Let's see where the main problems are … It's the Conference Centre fees that are the problem. The main conference room is €300 a day, so that's €600 for the two days. Extra rooms – they're €140 each. We've got four extra rooms, haven't we, so that's eight times €140, which is … €1,120.

M Giving a total of €1,720.

T This seems much more expensive than last year. Have you got last year's figures with you?

M No, but I remember that we only paid them about €1,500 last time. Do you want me to get in touch with them again?

T Good idea! Let's look at the other problem items. The speaker … €2,000 seems a lot! Who's coming?

M I think Eva Hanson has accepted. We had to find someone at the last minute because the original speaker dropped out.

T Oh, I saw her speak last month in Copenhagen. She's very good, actually.

M She's only staying for one night, so that keeps the hotel bill down a bit.

T OK. How did you calculate the cost of the conference packs?

M Well, last year, we had 300 participants. So I calculated for 350 this year. 350 times 2.5 is 875.

T It's quite a lot, isn't it? Can't we get that figure down a bit?

M I doubt it. We've already got a fairly big discount from the printers.

T Then, yes, that sounds fine. What's this cost for the multimedia equipment … €20 per hour?

M Yeah, I checked that with the Centre. All of the rooms have got standard equipment – computer, microphones, and sound system. And this is all included in the price of the rooms. But if we want an Internet connection, it will cost €20 per hour.

T I think we can do without the Internet. What do you think?

M I'll have to check and get back to you.

T Yes, do that. It's not a large sum, but we need to get these totals down somehow.

M As you said, it's the Conference Centre fees that have pushed us over budget.

T Yes, give them a ring and let me know what they say to you, OK?

10.5 The conference budget (*page 101*)

B = Bill   M = Michelle

B Bill Duffy, City Conference Centre.

M Bill, hi. It's Michelle here from CityActive.

B Hello! How are you? Nice to talk to you again. What can I do for you?

M Look, I wonder if I could check the quote you gave us for our Enterprise Days conference? It seems a lot higher than last year.

B What did we quote you?

M 300 for the main room and 140 for each additional room.

B Just a minute … Oh, I'm sorry! You've been quoted the commercial rates instead of the preferential rates. The preferential rates are only three per cent up on last year's.

M Well, that's good news. Can you fax them to me?

B No problem. I'll get them faxed right now. Sorry once again about that.

M Oh, these things happen. Thanks. And see you in a couple of weeks at the conference?

B Yes, I'll be around. Bye.

 10.6 (*page 102*)

C = Celia   E = Eva

C Good morning, Ms Hanson. I'm Celia Kirkpatrick from CityActive.

E How do you do? Please call me Eva.

C How do you do, Eva? I hope you haven't been waiting long?

E Not at all! Where I come from, we have a habit of arriving a little early. I was just sitting here admiring the view of the river.

C Yes, we're very proud of our river here in Dublin. Have you been to Ireland before?

E No, this is the first time. Everything is very green, isn't it?

C Yes, thanks to the rain we get, I suppose. By the way, would you like to borrow an umbrella?

E That's very kind of you. I haven't brought one with me.

C And how was your journey? No delays with the weather, I hope?

E It was fine. There were no problems at all, thanks.

C Well, shall we set off? I have a taxi waiting outside.

 10.7 Offers and invitations (*page 103*)

1

M1 Well, it's been a really productive day, hasn't it?

M2 Yes, it has. I've made some very promising contacts.

M1 Would you like to join us for dinner?

M2 Yes, I'd be delighted.

M1 Great. I'll see you in the hotel reception at about eight o'clock then.

2

F1 Have you been to Dublin before?

F2 Yes, I was here a couple of years ago, actually.

F1 We're thinking of doing some sight-seeing this evening. Are you free?

F2 Thanks, but I've got a lot of paperwork to do back at the hotel.

F1 Oh, I know what you mean. I'm hoping to do some work on the plane home tomorrow.

3

M Please, take a seat and make yourself comfortable.

F Thanks.

M Can I offer you a drink?

F A beer, please.

M OK, a nice cold beer coming up.

4

M I'm not sure what to order. There's a great selection.

F Have you tried the beef? It's a local speciality.

M I'm sorry, I'm a vegetarian.

F Oh, I had no idea. Well, they do some excellent vegetarian dishes here.

Module II

 11.1 A factory tour (*page 106*)

Good morning, everyone. I'm Alistair Patterson, and I'm responsible for health and safety here at the plant. Before we start the tour of the plant, please put on your jackets and the hard hats. Remember that you must always wear a hard hat when you are moving around the plant. OK, good. Is everyone ready? I'll take you around the main production lines first, then we'll visit the warehouse and we'll finish the tour back here in the main office building …

Now obviously, you mustn't smoke in the production area – in fact, there is no smoking allowed anywhere. Until last year, we had a special smoking area outside the office building, but now the whole plant is a no-smoking zone. As you can see, the main hazard here is the machinery. That's why you should always wear protective clothing. In fact, you can't enter this area if you aren't wearing jackets and hard hats …

Well, here we are in the warehouse. There are a lot of fire hazards in the warehouse, and so this area must be kept clean and tidy at all times. If you're working here, always put all waste material into the bins. There are fire extinguishers on the walls, and the fire exit is on the left. Can you see it? It's quite clearly marked. Please remember, we don't allow any food or drink in the warehouse area. You can only eat or drink in the canteen …

Now, just before we go back into the main office building, can you see the sign on the wall here? This is the main assembly point, where you should come if there is an emergency – a fire, for example. We do regular fire drills, and you should come here to this assembly point when you hear the fire alarm. This is the way we check that all employees and visitors are safe. That's why visitors must always sign in when they arrive at the plant, and sign out when they leave. We have to know who is on site at all times. Now, are there any questions …

 11.2 After the accident (*page 110*)

R = Ruth   L = Louise

R Hi, Louise. Have you got a few minutes? It's about the accident you had the other day.

L Yes, I'm not too busy at the moment. What do you need to know?

R You said that there were some mistakes in the copy of the accident report that you got. Can I check it with you?

L OK, fine. It was only a couple of things.

R Yes, but I think we should just check everything. It was on Tuesday, wasn't it? That was May the 5th.

L Yes, that's right, Tuesday the 5th.

R And it says here that it happened at three o'clock. Is that right?

L No, it isn't. It was just before lunch, so it was about one o'clock.

R OK, let's change that from three o'clock to one o'clock. And you fell over here in the office?

L I was right here at my desk. I was standing on that chair to get a file from on top of the cupboard.

R Really? And what happened? Did you lose your balance?

L Yes, I was trying to reach the file, and I lost my balance and fell off the chair. And the file fell off the cupboard and hit me on the head!

R Did you hurt yourself badly?

L No, I was really lucky – it was just a small cut on my head, nothing serious.

R And Jane gave you first aid?

L Yes, Jane gave me first aid, and then I went home. I took the afternoon off.

R OK. Now, is this the correct spelling of your surname, R–A–L–P–H?

L No, it's R–E–L–P–H.

R OK, let me change that as well. R–E–L–P–H. And you're the accounts assistant, aren't you?

L Yes, but it's new accounts, actually. We're a separate section.

R Oh yes, that's right. So, you were off work for the afternoon and …?

L Yes, just the afternoon. I came back the next day. That was yesterday morning. I'm fine.

R Aha … Now, last section … description of the accident. It says here 'the employee was standing on a chair to reach files which are kept on top of a cupboard. She was hit by a file which fell off the cupboard.' That's all correct, isn't it?

L Yes.

R Did you hurt yourself anywhere else, apart from your head?

L No.

R OK. Thanks for your time, Louise. Can you sign there to show that …

 11.3 After the accident *(page 111)*

A = Annie   **S** = Sally

A Sally, are you coming for lunch?

S Hi, Annie. Yes, but I just have to put these files away first.

A What are you doing?

S I have to sort all these old records and files, and decide which ones we should keep and which ones we can throw away.

A Wow, that's going to take you ages!

S I know. Plus, I've only done a few and I'm bored already.

A But why are you doing it? Whose idea was that?

S Oh, Mike says there isn't enough space to keep everything. He got a memo from the quality department. From now on, we mustn't keep files up on the top of cupboards like this.

A Oh, that's because Louise fell off a chair last week, isn't it? The man from maintenance came to check our office yesterday. He said we should buy those special stools to stand on when we can't reach things that are too high.

S Oh, yes, I know the stools you mean. We've got one somewhere, I think. Oh, I think I'll leave this for after lunch. Let's go.

A Come on then, I haven't got much time. I have to be back at two to meet the maintenance man again. He's going to fix some broken lights, or something …

 11.4 Exam spotlight, Listening Test Part Four
(page 114)

I = Interviewer   **R** = Richard

I I'm talking today to Richard Orson, who introduced an environment-friendly policy into his company, Personal Touch, which makes objects for the home. Welcome, Richard.

R Hello.

I Tell me, have you always promoted environment-friendly business practices?

R No, quite the opposite. I used to be convinced that it was bad for business. I thought that you couldn't be environment-friendly and maintain profits at the same time.

I So what changed your mind?

R Who, actually. It was my production manager, Peter Walker. He went to a meeting organised by our local business association. At the meeting, Peter heard about how cutting waste would benefit the environment, and it would also reduce costs. Well, afterwards, Peter started thinking more about the environment. And he attended some free seminars, where he learnt how to prepare an environment-friendly policy.

I What did you think about this?

R I didn't know very much about it. It was only when he had produced his policy that he showed it to me. But his arguments were convincing, and I had to listen to what he was saying.

I And what was he saying?

R That we could save money by cutting the amount of waste we produced.

I Well, it sounds easy in theory, but how did you decide where to cut waste?

R We brought in a company to assess our work procedures. That was in 2005. Then we asked them back in 2006 and again in 2007. The first report the company produced explained how we could reduce water consumption, use paper more carefully and cut photocopying, electricity and heating costs. We followed their suggestions, and in the first year, we were able to cut our energy bills by 17 per cent.

I That is a lot.

R Yes, but the biggest difference was in the amount of solid waste. We used to produce over 40 tonnes a year, and this has fallen to less than 30 tonnes.

I So you've made a cut of more than 25 per cent.

R That's right. Of course, the only way to achieve these reductions was to get the whole staff involved. We had some meetings early on with everyone to tell them what we intended to do. We appointed people, one person for each office, to check that the lights and PCs were switched off at the end of the day. We started a scheme to encourage staff to suggest new ways of reducing waste. And we provided bins for drinks cans to be recycled. This doesn't save us any money, but it does make staff more aware of environmental issues. Twice a year, we email all staff an update on what we have achieved, and we remind them of our targets for cutting waste. And finally, each department is monitored to see where cost savings can be made.

I And how much do you think you save in money terms?

R We save between three and four thousand pounds a year.

I That's not bad for a small company like yours.

R Exactly. And you know what? Every company could do what we've done, and make similar, or even greater savings. It just makes good business sense.

I Yes, I can see that. Well, thank you, Richard …

Module 12

 12.1 Job satisfaction *(page 116)*

I = Interviewer   **M** = Male speaker   **F** = Female speaker

1

I Excuse me. I'm asking people about their jobs. Would you change anything if you could?

F Oh yes, I'd like to work from home. I could quite easily do my job from home, without going to the office. I would save time and money if I didn't go to the office every day. And I could keep in touch with the office by email, or by phone. Of course, I'd have to go to the office occasionally, maybe once a week, or once a fortnight, but that wouldn't be so bad.

2

I Hello, I'm interviewing people about job satisfaction. Are you happy in your job?

M Yes, I am, most of the time.

I If you could change one aspect of your job, what would it be?

M I suppose I'd like to change the hours that I work. I'd prefer to work flexitime. The office hours are from 9am to 5pm, but at these times, the traffic is terrible. It takes me over an hour to get to work in the morning. If I could, I'd come to work earlier, around 7.30, and leave earlier, around 3.30, maybe. I would have more time with my children if I left work earlier.

3

I Hello. I'm interviewing people about job satisfaction. If you could change one thing in your job, what would it be?

F Only one thing? Well, I'm quite happy with everything … except for the holidays. In my company, everyone has to take their holidays in July or August. But this is when the schools close for the summer holidays, so all the families go away in these months, and everything is more expensive. If I could go on holiday in June, or September, I would pay less for my hotel room. That would be great. And, of course, the beaches wouldn't be so full of noisy children.

4

I Hello. I'm asking people about their jobs. Would you change anything in your job?

M I suppose there are some things I would change, if I could. For example, I'd like to have more responsibility, you know, and work more independently. At the moment, my boss doesn't let me do anything without his approval. I basically follow his orders, all the time. But I'd like to have the opportunity to use my experience and to show him what I can do.

I Thank you.

5

I Excuse me. I'm asking people about their jobs. Are you happy with your job?

M I haven't got a job. I'm unemployed.

 12.2 *(page 120)*

M = Maria   **J** = Jenny

M Hey, Jenny, it's Maria. Have you seen the Independent's job pages today? There's an advert for a PR coordinator at Système.

J Système? Wasn't that the company on the stand next to us at last month's Fashion Fair?

M Yes, that's the one. They're looking for a PR coordinator. It sounds pretty good. You should apply!

J What are they asking for?

M A degree and two years' experience in PR. So that's OK. You're a graduate, and you've been working here more than two years, haven't you?

J Yes, and I worked at L'Oréal before I came here.

M So your French is excellent, of course!

J Well, of course! What does the advert say about the actual job?

M Let's see … coordinating product launches … contacts with editors … writing articles for the media and planning PR strategies. Oh, and developing a website. What do you think? You could do all that!

J Well, I don't know a thing about websites! But the rest sounds really interesting, doesn't it?

M I'm sure you won't need any technical knowledge for the website – it would be more about the ideas for the site.

J Yes, you're probably right. What else do they want?

M You should be 'self-motivated and well-organised'. Well, I think you're both of those things. And it also says 'excellent IT and communication skills'.

J IT skills? Oh, I'm not sure about this.

M I'll tell you what, I'll email the page to you and you can read it yourself. I would apply if I were you – you're always saying how bored you are here!

J OK, then. Thanks, Maria. I'll have a look at it and we can talk about it at lunchtime.

12.3 A job interview *(page 122)*

I = Interviewer   **P** = Philip

I Good morning. Philip Barras, isn't it? Please take a seat.

P Yes, that's right. Good morning.

I Well, Philip, I see from your CV that you have some experience working in marketing.

P Yes, I have. I've worked in the marketing department of a large sportswear company for the last year.

I Can you tell me what you enjoy most about your current job?

P Yes, well … I've learnt a lot working with the sales and marketing team. I like the variety – you know, it's not always the same routine. And the people on the team are great – everyone works together and helps each other. I enjoy the satisfaction – when we meet our targets, I mean … it's very satisfying.

I And what about the routine tasks, the administration and so on?

P Yes, I have to do that too, but it's not a problem. I think every job has … well, a boring part. I'm quite well-organised, and actually I think it's important to do the routine things well too.

I I see. Now, why would you like to work here?

P Well, I think there are two reasons, mainly. The job looks very interesting – some of the areas are similar to what I do now, but with more responsibility. So I think it will be a challenge, but it will be exciting. And then … in a big company like this, I think I'll have more opportunities to learn new things.

I So, looking to the future, what would you like to be doing in a few years' time?

P I'd like to be in charge of my own account, and I'd like to manage my own team.

I OK, good. So what qualities do you bring to this particular position?

P Well, as you can see, I'm quite ambitious! I'm creative and enthusiastic – obviously I don't know everything about your products, but I do have a few ideas already about the marketing possibilities. I'm quite competitive – I like to meet targets and goals, as I said earlier.

I And what would you say were your weak points?

P Ah, that's a difficult question to answer. I suppose I can be impatient, sometimes.

I Hmm … Let's talk in a bit more detail about what this position involves …